The Mystic in the Theatre:

ELEONORA
DUSE

Eva Le Gallienne

Southern Illinois University Press
CARBONDALE AND EDWARDSVILLE

Feffer & Simons, Inc.
LONDON AND AMSTERDAM

Library of Congress Cataloging in Publication Data

Le Gallienne, Eva, 1899–
    The mystic in the theatre.

    (Arcturus books, AB108)
    1.   Duse, Eleonora, 1858–1924.   I.   Title.
[PN2688.D8L4   1973]   792′.028′0924   72–11975
ISBN 0–8093–0631–X

Acknowledgment is made to the editors of
Cornhill magazine, in whose pages an excerpt
from this book first appeared.

Reprinted by arrangement with Eva Le Gallienne
Arcturus Books Edition April 1973
This edition printed by offset lithography
    in the United States of America

The Mystic in the Theatre:

ELEONORA
DUSE

I

Eleonora duse.

From 1884 to 1924 that name stood for the most potent magic of which the theatre is capable.

To those who saw her—and, thank God, I am old enough to be one of them—that magic still remains undimmed and unsurpassed.

It always gives me a shock of surprise when young people—and others not so young—ask the question: "Who was *she?*" And many who know her name but never saw her act, eager to know more about her, ask: "What was she like?"—"How did she differ from other actors?"—"Why does that name conjure up such vivid memories?"

It is to try and answer some of these questions that this little book was written.

It is a commonplace to say that the art of acting is ephemeral. Unlike other artists, the great actor disappears, leaving no trace except in the hearts and minds of those who were members of his audience.

This is especially true of the great actors of the past, who lived and worked before motion pictures were brought to their present near-perfection. Nowadays it is possible to preserve, to some extent at least, a record of their achievements; though no mechanical device can ever, it seems to me, quite take the place of that mysterious communion between player and public, that sense of an experience directly shared, which gives to the living theatre its unique appeal.

I was no novice when, at the age of twenty-four, I first saw Duse play. I had already reached stardom, which, at a time when "starlets" had yet to be invented, implied a good deal of experience. And I had been fortunate in having spent my childhood in countries where the theatre was an integral part of people's lives; where it filled a definite need; where it was regarded not only as a place of entertainment and amusement but as a source of mental and spiritual well-being.

Such an attitude on the part of the public was bound to foster great playwrights; and their works, in turn, fostered great interpreters. I had seen many glorious performances. I had watched with wonder, awe and excitement such artists as Sarah Bernhardt, Réjane, Lucien Guitry, Julia Bartet, Alexander Moissi, Forbes-Robertson and Mrs. Fiske, to mention only a few of the giants who lived in those days.

Yet, somehow, as I grew older, I found myself

expecting even more from the theatre. I felt there might be heights, and depths, and mysterious hidden places which these people, marvellous though they were, had never quite succeeded in revealing fully.

Like Ibsen's Hilde Wangel, I wanted all these Master Builders to "do the impossible." My friends accused me of being too demanding, too intransigent, and I almost found myself agreeing with them.

Then, suddenly, I saw it happen—this thing that I had always dreamed of. I saw the stage take on an added dimension; I felt the vast audience grow still and sit as though mesmerized in the presence of a frail, worn woman who, with no apparent effort, through the sheer beauty of the truth within her, through the sheer power of her spirit, reached out to each one of us and held us all enthralled. I saw "the impossible" come true.

Of course, not everyone felt this way about Eleonora Duse. There were some who saw nothing on that stage but an old tired woman with white hair who didn't even take the trouble to hide the ravages of time with suitable make-up. Some were puzzled, and slightly resentful of the emotion which, in spite of themselves, affected them so strongly. Others, who came to the performance because they had been told it was a cultural "must" to see this woman who was hailed as the greatest actress of her day, were merely indifferent. But all, however unwillingly, found themselves held motionless and silent, as though in the grip of some inexplicable force.

Duse, the artist, was always controversial. And this was also true of Duse, the woman. Innovators are inevitably controversial. They are pioneers who lead the way into unfamiliar places. Just as Ibsen, Strindberg and Tchekov, brushing aside the traditional limitations of theatrical convention, were the first of the modern playwrights, so Duse was the first of the modern actors.

In the years following her death in 1924, several books were written about Duse. They are, for the most part, out of print. Many of them were written in foreign languages, and very few were ever translated into English.

With the exception of Lugné-Poë's volume of reminiscences, *Sous les Etoiles,* which contains a detailed, and very personal, account of his association with Duse, to the best of my knowledge no books have been written about her by an actor.

Perhaps, since I have spent over fifty years working in the medium through which Duse expressed her genius, I may be able to give a clearer picture of her acting than those who, no matter how deeply she may have impressed them, had no actual knowledge of her craft.

I was fortunate in having the opportunity to study her work closely. And even more fortunate in having known her personally. To me she was not only the greatest actress I have ever seen but a rare, generous, and most extraordinary human being.

If this little book succeeds, even to a small extent, in bringing her closer to those who never saw her, I shall be content.

And if, as I approach the end of my career, I can pass on to *les jeunes*—those young workers in whose hands the future of the theatre lies, to whom Duse always looked with such hope, tenderness and faith— even a tiny part of the immense help and inspiration she gave to me, I shall feel profoundly happy.

I I

"DONNE AUSSI À MON CORPS, O GÉNÉREUX *Rémunérateur, la splendide clarté, la prompte agilité, la pénétrante subtilité, la forte impassibilité.*"[1]

These were the first words Eleonora Duse asked me to read for her.

This was in 1923. I was twenty-four years old. She was sixty-five.

The above passage appears in a small book entitled *Prières de St. Thomas d'Aquin, traduites et présentées par M. l'Abbé Sertillanges*, and published at L'Art Catholique, 6 Place Saint-Sulpice, Paris, in the year 1920.

I can see now as though it were yesterday the light swift movement with which, as I prepared to take my leave of her, Duse went over to the window

---

[1] Most generous rewarder! Endow my body also with splendid clarity, with prompt agility, with penetrating subtlety, with strong impassibility.

sill where a pot of four-leaf clovers was standing; she plucked three of them and pressed them between the pages of the little book, then held it out to me with one of those rare smiles of hers which seemed to illumine not only her own face but the whole room, the whole universe.

The little book lies before me now, more than forty years after it passed from her hands to mine.

It is small and paperbound—approximately seven inches by five—and consists of one hundred and nine pages printed in bold clear type, beautifully set within wide margins, on a rather rough thick paper of an ivory tone. On the cover the title appears in red, in simple roman capitals of equal size. In the centre of the cover is a small design in black—a sheaf of wheat. The frontispiece is a formal, rather primitive wood-cut of Thomas Aquinas holding an open book which he seems to be offering, while his eyes, which look directly at you, urge rather than command you to obey and read. Beneath this woodcut the title appears again in the same red lettering as on the cover.

There is a short introduction in French by the Abbé Sertillanges. The prayers follow. The original Latin is printed on the left-hand page, and on the page opposite is the abbé's translation. The titles of the prayers and all the capital letters are in red.

The last paragraph on page seventy-five is the one

quoted above—the one Duse asked me to read for her. The top and bottom corners and the front of the page have been turned in and creased firmly so as to form a frame around these particular lines, which are alone visible, the rest of the text being covered by the folded corners. As if this were not enough to emphasize the value and importance of the passage, it is strongly marked on the inner margin by a vigorous thumb-nail.

Other markings throughout the little book show that it had been thoroughly read and pondered over.

On page twenty-seven the upper right-hand corner has been turned down to mark the following verse:

> *"Aux saintes solennités que nos joies soient égales,*
> *Que du profond des coeurs les acclamations*
>   *résonnent,*
> *Que toutes choses anciennes s'écartent et que tout*
>   *soit nouveau:*
> *Les coeurs, les voix, les oeuvres.*[2]

This would appeal to one whose gaze was always focussed on new frontiers, wider horizons—who believed in youth and whose art and spirit were ever young.

[2] May our joys resemble holy ceremonies,
From the depths of our hearts let acclamations ring,
Let us discard the old, that all things may be new:
Our hearts, our voices, and our works.

On page eighty-three the upper and lower corners have been turned in to frame the whole text, which reads:

"*Que toute joie me fatigue qui est sans Toi, et que je ne désire rien en dehors de Toi. Que tout travail, Seigneur, me soit agréable qui est pour Toi, et que tout repos insupportable qui est sans Toi. Donne-moi souvent de porter mon coeur vers Toi et, quand je faiblis, de peser ma faute avec douleur, avec un ferme propos de me corriger.*

"*Rends-moi, Seigneur mon Dieu, obéissant sans contradiction, pauvre sans défection, chaste sans corruption, patient sans protestation, humble sans fiction, joyeux sans dissipation, triste sans abattement, grave sans rigidité, actif sans légèreté, animé de ta crainte sans découragement, sincère sans duplicité, faisant le bien sans présomption, reprenant le prochain sans hauteur, l'édifiant de parole et d'éxample sans faux-semblants.*"[3]

[3] May all joy that is without Thee fill me with weariness, may I desire nothing apart from Thee. May all work done for Thee, Lord, be pleasing to me, and all rest which is without Thee insupportable. Grant that I may often uplift my heart to Thee, and when I weaken, let me weigh my fault with sorrow, with a firm resolve to mend it.

Make me, my Lord and my God, obedient without contradiction, poor without defection, chaste without corruption, patient without protestation, humble without fiction, joyous without dissipation, sad without dejection, grave without rigidity, active without frivolity, filled with fear of Thee without discouragement, sincere without duplicity, doing good

Between the next two pages are the four-leaf clovers; brown, dry, but still perfect in form—just as Duse placed them there so many years ago; and two lines are heavily underscored with a lead pencil:

"Donne-moi, Seigneur Dieu, un coeur libre que nulle violente passion ne subjugue . . . une intelligence qui te connaisse. . . ."[4]

Two more passages are marked in the little book. On page eighty-seven, a pencil not being available, the outer margin has been torn into the lines:

"Je Te loue, je Te glorifie, je Te bénis, mon Dieu, pour les immenses bienfaits que Tu m'as accordés á moi indigne."[5]

And the corner of page one hundred and seven has been turned down to indicate the importance of the whole, and we read:

> *5. Fréquente avec amour la cellule, si tu veux être introduit dans le cellier à vin.*
> *6. Montre-toi aimable à tous.*
> *7. Ne t'enquiers aucunement des actions d'autrui.*

---

without presumption, reproving my neighbour without haughtiness, edifying him by word and example without false pretences.
[4] Grant me, my Lord and my God, a free heart which no violent passion may subdue . . . an intelligence aware of Thee. . . .
[5] I praise Thee, I glorify Thee, I bless Thee, my God, for the immense favours Thou hast bestowed on me, unworthy as I am.

> 8. *Ne sois pas trop familier avec personne, car l'excès de familiarité engendre le mépris et fournit occasion de s'arracher à l'étude.*
>
> 9. *Ne te mêle nullement des paroles et des actes des séculiers.*
>
> 10. *Fuis par-dessus tout les démarches inutiles.*
>
> 11. *Songe à imiter la conduite des saints et des hommes de bien.*
>
> 12. *Ne regarde pas à celui qui parle, mais tout ce que tu entends de bon, confie-le à ta mémoire.*
>
> 13. *Ce que tu lis et entends, fais de sorte de le comprendre.*[6]

It may seem strange that such things should have been marked by an actress—the greatest actress of her time. The fact is that Eleonora Duse was also a mystic.

[6]
5. Cultivate with love the seclusion of your cell, if you wish to gain admittance to the wine cellar.
6. Be loving-kind to all.
7. Do not scrutinize other people's actions.
8. Be not too familiar with anyone, for excessive familiarity breeds contempt, and distracts one from study.
9. Have nothing to do with the words and actions of worldly men.
10. Avoid all profitless occupations.
11. Strive to imitate the behaviour of the saints and of worthy men.
12. Store up in your memory all the good that you hear, regardless of its source.
13. Whatever you read and hear, make sure that you understand it.

By this I do not mean that she was religious in the ordinary sense of the word; nor did she obey the rules of any specific church or creed. In her own words:

"Tant que la sensibilité reste seule intéréssée, je suis gagnée. Dès que l'intransigeance de la doctrine et l'aspect purement écclésiastique entrent en jeu, je suis rebelle."[7]

Duse was as great an individualist as St. Teresa of Avila, who wrote:

"It is no light cross to submit our intelligence to someone who hasn't very much himself. Personally, I've never succeeded and I don't believe one ought to do it."

D. H. S. Nicholson in his *Mysticism of St. Francis of Assisi* says:

"He [the mystic] is no more bound down to a particular sphere of usefulness or to a particular type of action than he is limited to the tenets of a particular creed: the essentials of mysticism underlie and vitalize all creeds as for the mystic they spiritualize all that he does in any branch of life . . . in the unalterable belief that all roads that are followed in love and aspiration lead finally to Him."

And Edouard Schneider quotes Madame Lucia Casale as saying of Duse:

[7] When moral sensibility alone is in question, I am won; but as soon as doctrinal intransigence and a purely ecclesiastical point of view enter in, I rebel.

"D'une façon générale elle avait la religion des oeuvres d'art et, bien légitimement, pensait que l'artiste possède en lui quelque chose de divin."[8]

In calling Duse a mystic, I do not mean either that she was what is known as a "moral" woman. As Havelock Ellis says in *The Dance of Life:* "We fall into sad confusion if we take it for granted that a mystic is what we conventionally term a 'moral man.' "

I do mean, however, that she was a seeker after God, that she was a servant of God, that she worshipped God; and that she sought, and served, and worshipped Him in and through and by her work.

Ten years after her debut in the theatre—at the age of fourteen—she played Juliet, and it seems that for the first time she experienced a real sense of dedication—the "state of grace." In d'Annunzio's book *Il Fuoco,* Perdita, speaking of her first performance of Juliet, says, in words that are admittedly Duse's: "Each word before leaving my lips seemed to have passed through all the warmth of my blood. There was no fibre in me which did not give forth an harmonious sound. Ah, grace! The state of grace! Each time it is given me to touch the summit of my art I recover that unspeakable abandonment."

And Count Primoli in describing the same occasion

---

[8] In general, her religion was the work of art, and quite legitimately she believed that the artist has in him something of the divine.

writes: "It was her revelation, in which she found grace."

Having once experienced this "revelation," she saw the theatre and her work in it in a new light, and though many years of misery and what mystics would call "dryness" of spirit lay ahead before she would again be permitted to "touch the summit" of her art, she now knew that she was one of the chosen, that she was a "messenger," and that her work was an act of service.

Duse was by nature a contemplative. Though her childhood must of necessity have been spent surrounded by a considerable number of people, the members of that humble company of actors into which she was born, she seems always to have been lonely— perhaps aloof is a better word. The following description, by Count Primoli, of her behaviour after her first triumphant performance as Juliet is indicative:

"Trop suréxcitée pour rentrer, la jeune fille se mit à errer a travers les rues; son père la suivait sans lui parler, respectant son silence . . . Et l'enfant marcha ainsi pendant des heures. Elle marchait devant elle, allant vers l'avenir, tout à son rêve."[9]

---

[9] Too overwrought to go home, the young girl wandered through the streets, followed by her father, who respected her silence and did not speak to her. . . . The child walked on for hours. She walked straight ahead, looking towards her future, possessed by her dreams.

There is no trace here of the kind of excitement, the personal jubilation, of the ordinary young actress after her first taste of success. Duse's behaviour was more that of a young priest who has just officiated at a solemn communion.

And indeed she never seems to have been driven by the ordinary ambition for personal fame. There were many times when she felt remote from the theatre, almost alien to it, when she thought of it with distaste, and of her dedication to it as an intolerable burden. E. A. Reinhardt in his excellent *Life of Eleonora Duse* quotes a letter written by her in 1884 at the age of twenty-six to her friend the Marchese d'Arcais. Duse had fled from the theatre, as she frequently throughout her life felt compelled to do, and was staying in a little village in the Piedmontese mountains. In this letter we read such phrases as: "When I think that I must go back to that distracted and chaotic life . . ." "I have almost forgotten the stage. I could almost say that to me it is as if I had never acted in the theatre. Acting—what an ugly word! If it were merely a question of acting, I feel that I could never have done it, and could never do it again."

If it were not just "a question of acting," what was it?

Duse had an immense reverence for art in all its

forms, and to her the art of the theatre was in no way inferior to music, painting, sculpture or poetry. She saw it ideally as a synthesis of all the arts combined. She saw it as a great force capable of spreading beauty and understanding, whose function it was to quicken in the minds and hearts of the people an appreciation of the nobility of suffering, to awaken in them a sense of the sublime; to rouse them from their torpor and through a heightening of the emotions make them aware of the mystery and wonder of the human spirit.

To her the theatre was still closely allied to religion, from which it originally sprang.

It might be objected that the plays in which she appeared during the years of her greatest triumphs were in no way "sublime"; that such works as *La Femme de Claude*, *La Dame aux Camélias*, *Denise*, *Magda*, *The Second Mrs. Tanqueray* and countless others, were merely theatre pieces designed to entertain the public with vicarious thrills and decidedly worldly passions. But she succeeded by the peculiar quality of her genius in raising them to a high spiritual level; she was like a crucible in which the sufferings and sins of all these various women were sublimated into the pure essence of pity, terror and pain. Her acting—to use that "ugly word"—was sacrificial; it was as though each time she played she immolated herself upon an altar.

This reckless annihilation of self was what made

her unique among actresses. In a profession in which the ever-increasing exploitation of self is the main objective, her aim throughout her life was the elimination of self—the "self-naughting" of the mystic—in order that she should become merely an instrument by which the Universal Self could be expressed. "I would fain be to the Eternal Goodness what a man's hand is to a man."[1]

It must not be thought this was an easy task that Duse had set herself; and indeed for many years she was herself probably unaware of having undertaken it. It was a slow and gradual process.

By nature she was violent, passionate, rebellious—yes, even ruthless. But the same could be said of Teresa of Avila. In her extreme youth Duse was certainly less frivolous and worldly than the great Spanish mystic; but this was probably due to the different circumstances of their birth. In both women the singleness of purpose that soon appeared in them was inevitably related to a strong sense of ego, and in its earlier manifestations it must have given the impression of a willfulness, an inflexibility, that could easily be construed by the outsider as intolerable self-importance.

Mystics—far less saints—are rarely made of amiable stuff. There must first be an ego to destroy if

[1] *Theologia Germanica.*

[1 9]

one is to set about destroying it. And if "ego" is synonymous with "devil" in the mystic's vocabulary, the line between devil and saint is very fine. People who are born even-tempered, placid and untroubled—secure from violent passions or temptations to evil—those who have never needed to struggle all night with the Angel to emerge lame but victorious at dawn, never become great saints.

So it was a long and difficult road Duse had to travel before the spiritual force that was in her finally crystallized and gave her the unique quality which drew vast audiences to see her as a frail, prematurely aged woman during her last appearances on the stages of the world, and sent the more sensitive among these audiences away silent, inspired and reverent as though they had indeed been in the presence of a messenger of God.

There were of course many who scoffed, many who saw only the white hair and the worn face; some who felt cheated at the lack of histrionics, who even failed to perceive—apart from the quality of the woman herself—the almost incredible technical virtuosity; a virtuosity so great as to seem non-existent.

Indeed, in order to recognize Duse's unequalled mastery of her craft, it was necessary to see her play the same part several times; each thought seemed to spring freshly from her mind and spirit to take form in words never spoken before; each movement seemed to flow spontaneously and inevitably from a situation undreamed of until that very moment; yet each thought, each word, each slightest movement was part of a highly disciplined concept of the role and of the play, executed with such truth and such superlative skill that it seldom varied from one performance to the next. Yet the process was so subtle that it was often said—and many critics suffered from this illusion—that Duse "had no technique" but played on the "inspiration of the moment."

However, quite apart from this aspect of her work, which made her the greatest exponent of the actual "art of acting" of her time, there was the other element—that intangible "something else," as Arthur Symons calls it in his book on Duse: "It is that something else, divined underneath all she says, and all that she looks, which gives her incomparable power over her audience." It was this "something else" that had always set her apart from other famous actresses, and roused in those attuned to it a feeling akin to worship. And of Duse the woman, apart from the artist, Matilde Serao wrote: "My friendship for Duse was a veritable religion."

But like all great artists Duse was a creature of many facets. I believe she would have considered her most important—perhaps her *only* important—

achievement, the gradual victory over her own temperament, the annihilation of her own ego. "She was the artist of her own soul," to quote Symons again; and this work on her own soul was certainly not undertaken primarily—if at all—with the theatre in mind. The pattern of her own spiritual evolution would have been the same no matter what her circumstances or her occupation. She was probably all unaware at first of the links between the studies of mysticism which more and more engrossed her, and her work in the theatre. But since the texture of her own being was always inextricably bound up with her playing, it was inevitable that the two should end in fusion. And, given the premise that the greatest and purest art must be impersonal, why should the "self-naughting" of the mystic not add a potent factor to the art of acting too? Once she became aware of being a channel for some higher force, would it not then be logical to wish to clear that channel, to the fullest extent humanly possible, of all the trivia and impedimenta of self, in order that that force might sweep through unimpaired by the smallest "lump of stinking ego," to use the words of the anonymous author of *The Cloud of Unknowing?*

Perhaps the artist-mystic has a special danger to combat—and the greater the artist the greater the danger—for as Aquinas says: "The very perception of the angels, in other words, exposed them to the danger of the gifted; the danger of enchantment with the splendour of the gifts to the denial of the Giver."

Of all the artistic media, surely the theatre, with its glorification of the human personality, the actual presence of cheering applauding crowds, the exaggerated, often fantastic, eulogies splashed with such thoughtless prodigality in a thousand newspaper columns, the vast sums of money that successful actors earn, the often fulsome adulation to which they are exposed, surely the theatre is the least propitious environment for the potential mystic.

Duse did not escape these pitfalls. She had many enemies, and often deserved them. Many people thought her—with good reason—intolerant, spoiled and selfish. The members of her companies either adored her—though usually at a distance, for her naturally aloof nature was not conducive to familiarity —or found her cold and distant, and her wildly fluctuating moods disconcerting. But while as a woman she may have been capricious, as an artist she was invariably consistent. Speaking of her earliest triumph in the words of d'Annunzio's Perdita quoted above, it is indicative that she uses the phrase "each time *it is given me* to touch the summit of my art"; and many years later, speaking of the amazing reception she received in Turin on her return to the stage in 1921, she said to Edouard Schneider: "*Le grand succès du premier soir de Turin, à l'heure du retour! Certes, tout le*

*monde était ému. Moi seule ne l'était pas. Ce suc-
cés allait à quelque chose de plus grand que moi, pas-
sait au-dessus de ma tête, s'adressait à une force que
je représentais, mais qui n'était pas moi. . . ."*[2]

Whenever she gave a superlatively great performance she never felt that *she* had given it, but rather
that it "had been given her" to give—"*à moi indigne.*"
At those times when she reached "the summit of her
art" it was like an answer to a prayer; and the prayer
was never "let me play well for my own sake," but
rather simply "let me serve, for the greater glory of
God!"

[2] The great success of that first night in Turin, at the hour
of my return! Everyone was moved. I alone was not. This
success belonged to something far greater than me; it was way
above me; it was directed to a force which was not me—I
was merely its representative.

III

IT WAS PROBABLY INEVITABLE THAT ELEONORA Duse should have become an actress. Indeed the circumstances of her birth practically made it mandatory. She started acting at the age of four. She had no choice in the matter. Her entire family, with the exception of her mother, was part of the humble itinerant company of players who struggled painfully to earn their living on the stage, seeking—though unsuccessfully—to emulate the triumphs of Eleonora's grandfather, the famous Luigi Duse, who was the first of his name to abandon the life of the sea for that of the theatre. This was his father's idea: he wished his son to become a respectable civil servant dedicated to a life of security and order, and had him suitably educated accordingly.

But "security" made Luigi restless. The magic of the sea was in his blood. The Civil Service was not for him. So he turned to the theatre, where he found magic too. The stages of the old wooden playhouses of his day replaced the decks of the wooden ships his fore-fathers had sailed on.

His success with audiences was instantaneous and he soon founded his own company—the Compagnia Duse—and became an idol of the public all over Italy.

There is a little street in Chioggia, a seaport just south of Venice, which is named after him: the Calle Duse.

At his insistence his sons all became actors, and, with one exception, married actresses: the Compagnia Duse was a family affair. Unfortunately none of them inherited their father's genius, and, after his death, the Compagnia Duse became a third-rate group of travelling players, fighting against unimaginable conditions in the most bitter poverty. Into this life Eleonora Duse was born on October 3rd, 1858. She did not choose to be an actress, she was forced to be one.

When a small child was needed to play the part of Cosette in *Les Misérables* it was logical that four-year-old Eleonora should be made to serve the purpose. This was the beginning. It was the first of a long series of varied characters—many of them mature far beyond her years—which she acted without enthusiasm, with no conscious sense of vocation, but simply because it was part of the routine of living.

It would be impossible for young actors today,

pampered and protected as they are by union mini-
mums and regulations, accustomed to the comforts of
modern transportation, to imagine the hardships such
a travelling company endured.

In many parts of Italy there were no railroads
until the '70s, and the Compagnia Duse moved from
one small town to another in a wagon, many of the
actors walking along beside it. The inns they could
afford were cold and dirty, and the theatres were cold
and dirty too. The young women of the company
swept the stages themselves, cleaned the dressing
rooms, washed and mended the old costumes and, now
and then, when there was money to spare, concocted
new ones.

I remember Duse describing to me her arrival in a
small town just before dawn. She and her father and
the rest of the company had walked all through the
night. It was too early to go to the inn, so they washed
their hands and faces in the fountain of the public
square and sat down to rest on the stone benches, waiting for the day. Across the square Duse saw a small
girl sitting alone. She went over to her, sat down beside
her and took her hand. They did not speak but sat
there together hand in hand until the sun began to
rise, and were comforted by one another's presence.
The girl's name was Déjanira. "You remind me of
her," Duse said to me. "I have not thought of her for

many, many years. She was my first friend—my only childhood friend—I loved her." For several days Déjanira stayed with the troupe of actors—no one knew where she came from or where she was going. The two children shared whatever meagre food was offered and shared a cot at night. Then the company moved on and Duse never saw her friend again. She took my hand and was silent for a while, remembering. The vivid simplicity with which Duse told the story—with no comment on the hardships she described, for they were the commonplaces of her existence at that time—made me feel I had actually been there and shared in the experience. I felt the patient, almost fatalistic, acceptance of harsh conditions; the constant moving on from one town to another, with no home to rest in, no thought of the future, only the knowledge of a job that must be done in order to eat and sleep with a roof over one's head.

This gruelling apprenticeship, in which there was no time for thoughts of personal aggrandizement, and in which natural reserve and timidity of temperament had to be subjugated to the necessities of the job in hand, was undoubtedly a potent factor in giving Duse an early command over the fundamental technique of acting, so that by her middle twenties, when she at last began to emerge from obscurity, she was already in full control of her craft; and it explains the curious anachronism that revealed this least "theatrical" of actors as the greatest craftsman of her time.

The only one of Luigi's sons who seems to have inherited a glimmer of his father's talent was Enrico; when Luigi died he became head of the company, together with the actor Lagunaz. Duse's father, Alessandro, disliked the theatre and would have preferred to be a painter; but, at the insistence of the great Luigi, he too became an actor—though never a good one. He was a quiet, rather melancholy man, who seems to have understood his daughter's reserved and brooding nature. Duse's mother, Angelica Cappelletto, was not an actress—though until she became too ill to work she was put into small parts, for everyone had to be of use. She died, of tuberculosis, when Duse was fourteen—soon after that performance of Juliet which was the first important milestone in her life. She could not have been more than eighteen when she lost her father, and then her uncle—so before she was twenty years old Duse was quite alone.

It was hard for her to make her way. Not only was she so poor that she appeared badly dressed and half starved, but the flame of aspiration, the sense of dedication that had sprung to life on that evening in Verona when she "found grace," gave her an aura of apartness. To the managers and actors of the second-rate theatres in which she sought employment, she must have seemed queer, contemptible—perhaps a little frightening. Her singleness of purpose, her passionate faith in what the theatre could and should be, made these crude, commonplace showfolk uncomfortable. To them the stage was simply a way to make a living, and their dreams for it were dreams for themselves: to be rich and famous; to hear the applause of the crowds; to be able to lord it over their less fortunate comrades. Any thought of service to an art struck them as ludicrous.

Duse suffered unspeakable humiliations. She hated the cheap theatrical tricks, the empty melodramatic gestures, the false intonations imposed on her by the directors. It was essential that she keep her job, so for the most part she was silent, but they sensed her rebellion and resented it. She was told repeatedly that the stage was no place for her and advised to seek some other occupation. She had no friends, her colleagues despised and ridiculed her; but nothing could weaken her faith; nothing could stifle that unerring instinct which told her that while this was not *her* theatre, some day she must and would find it.

She went from one engagement to another, playing small parts for starvation wages. Then, one evening in Naples, the leading lady fell ill and Duse had to go on as Maia in Augier's *Les Fourchambault*. A well-known actor, Giovanni Emanuel, was in the audience. He was a man of taste who had the courage to think along original lines and who detested the banal, hackneyed conventions which prevailed in the Italian theatre of that time. He saw something in the "little Duse" which startled and intrigued him. With the help of the Princess Santa Buono, a rich patron of the arts, he started his own company in Naples, at the Teatro dei Fiorentini, with the famous actress Giacinta Pezzana as his star and twenty-one-year-old Eleonora Duse as his leading ingénue.

Duse was fortunate in this engagement. Emanuel had the good sense to leave her alone—he was not afraid of her "queerness" and her individuality. In this he may have been influenced by Pezzana—a generous-minded perceptive woman, no longer young —who was the first person to realize fully Duse's potentialities. She prophesied that some day Duse would become "a very great actress."

It was due to Pezzana that Duse enjoyed her first real success, as Thérèse in Zola's *Thérèse Raquin*. In spite of the Grand-Guignolesque quality of the play— with its theme of illicit love, murder and final retribution—Eleonora acted with such violent truth, such simple passion, that Pezzana, as Madame Raquin, was inspired by her young colleague, and played as never before. Far from being jealous, she delighted in the acclaim Duse received—it is not true that older actresses must inevitably resent young ones—and Duse, herself so generous in later years, never forgot the help Pezzana gave her.

This first success, and Pezzana's faith in her, gave her courage; she became less shy, less retiring; she was no longer so afraid of people, and in the young writer Matilde Serao she found a life-long friend, one to whom she could pour out her most secret thoughts and aspirations.

Then she fell in love.

There was always an element of worship in Duse's love affairs—and she had many. There was never anything casual or trivial in these relationships. Each one seemed like a step that led her upward to greater mental and spiritual development. There was joy, of course —the joy of life flowed through her strongly, even violently—but it was never merely pleasure. The gravity of her nature must have protected her during the hard years she lived through after the death of her father, when she was quite alone. The theatre now is no easy place for a young girl, but at that time it must have been a rare thing for one to remain untouched and pure until she *chose*. But, having chosen, she offered herself freely and as though with dedication to her first lover.

Martino Cafiero was considerably older than Eleonora; he was a well-known writer—clever, experienced, a man of taste, but vain and totally unscrupulous. His knowledge of art and literature was inexhaustible; he opened innumerable doors for the "little Duse," fed her innate craving for beauty in all its forms: poetry, drama, painting, sculpture, music. He pointed out the glories of the countryside round Naples, and introduced her to refinements in food and wines, the myriad graces of living of which she had hitherto been ignorant. She looked up to him as to some godlike creature, and worshipped him.

As might have been expected, Cafiero soon became bored with the grave intensity of Duse's passion. He was only too relieved when the season at the Teatro dei Fiorentini came to an end, and both Pezzana and Duse were engaged by Cesare Rossi to appear in Turin.

The affair ended for Duse in heartbreak and disaster, culminating in the death of the little boy to whom she gave birth after her lover had deserted her.

After the birth and death of her child, Duse went back to Turin and rejoined the Cesare Rossi Company. Pezzana had left, and Rossi gave Duse all the leading parts. Though he was puzzled and often irritated by her, he had vision enough to recognize her genius, and was wise enough to allow her free rein. But Duse was not happy in the stuffy, trite melodramas she was obliged to play. There were moments when she was on the point of abandoning the stage and turning to other channels—though none presented itself clearly. This travesty of the theatre was not what she had been born to serve.

Her life was soon complicated by Rossi's unwelcome attentions. When this situation became intolerable, she escaped into marriage as into a refuge.

Duse's husband was a member of the company, a mediocre actor, but good, kind and dependable. She did not love Tèbaldo Checchi, but was grateful for his devotion and protection. Rossi appears to have been decent enough to bear no grudge against her, and husband and wife continued to play in his theatre.

Matilde Serao wrote of this time: "How much whispered slander and open ridicule fell about Tebaldo Checchi's ears on account of this marriage! In secret he was called 'the pimp.' And openly 'the leading lady's husband.' He knew, listened to it all, shrugged his shoulders and laughed. Yes, he was the leading lady's husband; but he was also the watchful protector of that chosen creature. . . . He stood before her, protected her with his body and took on himself all those troubles which are unavoidable for a rising actress. Then there were people who condoled with Eleonora Duse over such an ordinary and undistinguished husband; but she drew her brows together and quickly silenced those unwelcome sympathizers. With a word, with a gesture, she put a stop to those who talked against her husband; only she and the very few who

were intimate with her knew what a touching solici-
tude for his wife he was capable of."

In 1882 their child was born, a daughter, Enrichetta. Not wishing to subject her to the difficult conditions of theatre life, Duse decided to leave her in
charge of a couple whose kindness and honesty had
been recommended to her. They lived not far from
Turin and Duse visited Enrichetta as often as her
work allowed her to do so.

Then came another milestone in Duse's career: she
saw great acting for the first time. Sarah Bernhardt,
already at the height of her spectacular fame, came to
play a brief engagement at Rossi's theatre. Duse attended all her performances and was profoundly
moved. In her own words: "She came irradiated by
her great aureole, her world-wide fame. And as if
by magic the theatre was suddenly filled with movement and life. . . . To me it was as if with her approach all the old, ghostly shadows of tradition and of
an enslaved art faded away to nothing. It was like an
emancipation. She was there, she played, she triumphed, she took possession of us all, she went
away . . . but like a great ship she left a wake behind her . . . and for a long time the atmosphere
she had brought with her remained in the old theatre.
A woman had achieved all that! And in an indirect
way I, too, felt myself released; I, too, felt that I had

the right to do what seemed right to me, and something quite different from what I had previously been compelled to do. And actually they did not interfere with me after that. She played *La Dame aux Camélias:* how wonderful! I went every evening and cried."

And so the impact of the great *"cabotine de génie,"* as the French sometimes affectionately—and quite accurately—describe *"la grande Sarah,"* was instrumental in freeing a younger and very different artist. Though Duse admired her passionately (and in spite of Sarah's shocking treatment of her in later years, this admiration never failed), she knew that Sarah's ways were not her ways; the daring of the great French actress, far from tempting her to imitation, stimulated her to be even more *herself.*

This experience was a definite turning point in Duse's work: "It was like an emancipation." From then on her own powers began to grow and strengthen. Success such as she had never known came to her. In *La Princesse de Bagdad,* in *La Femme de Claude* (both plays by Alexandre Dumas fils) she scored veritable triumphs, not only in Turin but in Rome—the most critical and skeptical of all Italian cities.

What pleased her most, and gave her the most courage, was that these plays had met with failure in previous performances both in France and in Italy. She had succeeded by her playing, which Symons has called "the antithesis of acting," in bringing them to life. In 1884 Dumas fils finished another play especially for her—*Denise*—in which she made another triumphant success.

But success, far from lulling her into complacent contentment, only spurred her to new efforts. Her cry was always "I must work, I must learn!" To the end of her life, when for many years she had been acclaimed the greatest artist in the theatre, her cry was still "I must work, I must learn!" In the last telegram she sent before her death in Pittsburgh in April 1924, which lies before me now, she said: *"Vous trouverez une nouvelle force dans le nouvel effort."*

She welcomed the applause and cheers of the crowd because they were a proof to her of work well done, but they were forgotten as soon as they were over, and what remained was the challenge, the constant aspiration to perfect herself as an ever finer, more sensitive, more revealing instrument with which to serve. "I must work, I must learn!"

In 1885 Duse embarked on a South American tour. It was the first time she had left Italy. The engagement started in Rio de Janeiro, and it began disastrously. The play was *Fédora*. The theatre was enormous. Duse wrote her friend Matilde Serao: "A complete failure for your little Nenella—a huge, huge theatre—I felt quite small and helpless . . . I should have had to say 'I love you' in the same voice as one usually says 'Begone!' for my voice to have carried."

The next day she played *Denise*, to an almost empty house; but people began to be aware that something unusual was happening on that vast stage. By the third performance, which was *Fernande*, Duse had begun to adjust herself to the "huge theatre," and from then on her success was assured. "Your little Nenella won," she wrote Serao.

This tour was fateful in many ways. Tebaldo Checchi knew that Duse had never loved him, and now he realized she had fallen in love with someone else—her leading man, the well-known actor Flavio Andò. Duse fought against her feelings, for she respected and admired Checchi, and was intensely grateful to him. The thought of hurting him was anguish to her—but she had to be honest with him and with herself. She told him the truth. There was of course no possibility of divorce—they were both Italians and both Catholics—but they agreed on a separation. Checchi resigned from the company and decided not to return to Italy. He had made many friends in South America and through their influence obtained a position in the diplomatic corps of the Argentine republic.

Shortly after Duse's return to Italy in 1886, she

broke with Cesare Rossi and formed her own company—the Drammatica Compagnia della Città di Roma. Flavio Andò stayed on as director and leading man. Their professional association lasted for ten years, but their personal relationship was brief. Duse soon found that Andò, like many another matinee idol, "*était beau mais il était bête.*"[1]

Cafiero, in spite of the sorrow he had brought her, had an intellect she could look up to; he had awakened her, not only as a woman, but as an artist; he had opened her eyes to beauty in every form and had roused in her an unquenchable desire to read, to learn, to make up for her almost total lack of education. And this pattern was to repeat itself in all the great loves of Duse's life.

The greatest of these, contrary to the popular legend, was not d'Annunzio, but the poet and composer Arrigo Boito, creator of *Mefistofele*, *Nerone*, and the libretti for Verdi's *Otello* and *Falstaff*—a great intellectual and a man of genius.

Duse had met Boito briefly before leaving for South America, but it was not until 1887 that they became close. Now that she had all the responsibilities of her own theatre, now that she was artistically emancipated and on her own, she felt the need of guidance and inspiration, and Boito seemed to have

---

[1] He was beautiful but dumb.

been sent to her by some higher power—"the saint," she called him. He used to say to her: "Up, up towards the vision!" They lived in what Duse herself described as *"un febbrone d'arte."*[2]

As her own manager she was free to search for plays of more originality and power than those Cesare Rossi had imposed upon her. It is true that she kept many of her popular successes in her repertoire, for it was necessary to play to full houses to keep her company together, but she added to the plays of Dumas fils and Sardou (whom she particularly despised) works by young Italian playwrights—Verga, Praga, Giacosa and many others—and revived some of Goldoni's comedies—that great Venetian, neglected for many years, whose *La Locandiera* she made peculiarly her own. She discovered, and dared to produce, a controversial play by Renan, *L'Abbèsse de Jouarre*, which, while never a popular success, won her much critical acclaim. She added Pinero's *The Second Mrs. Tanqueray* to her repertoire, and at last she turned once more to Shakespeare, playing *Antony and Cleopatra* in Boito's adaptation, as well as *Romeo and Juliet*. She introduced Ibsen to Italy with her production of *A Doll's House.*

Her fame, as an innovator as well as a great actress, began to spread all over Europe, and in 1890 she was invited to play at the Little Theatre (Maly) in St.

[2] A fever of art.

Petersburg. I remember Duse saying to me many years later (in 1923), "Of all the audiences I have ever played to, the Russian audiences are best!" She never forgot their extraordinary warmth, their uninhibited enthusiasm, their sensitive perception. "They really understood what I was trying to do," she told me.

A theatrical agent, Tänczer, wrote to her from Vienna suggesting she should play a season there. She hesitated, for she had heard of the hypercritical spirit of the Viennese, who considered themselves the supreme judges of everything theatrical. But the Austrian author, Hermann Bahr, who had seen her play *La Femme de Claude* in St. Petersburg, wrote her a persuasive letter urging her to come, and she decided to take the risk. This was in 1892. She opened at the Karl Theater—one of the least fashionable in Vienna—in *La Dame aux Camélias*. There were not many people in the house, but those who were there—including the critics—felt they had been enriched by an entirely new experience, that a new kind of theatre had been revealed to them. The reviews were bewildered, frantic, ecstatic—the houses were packed from then on.

Duse returned to Russia, then went to Berlin, then to Vienna again—the people went mad about her everywhere, and the critics wrote as though they had never seen acting before.

She was now famous all over Europe—though she had still to play in London and Paris—and when

Tänczer offered to arrange an American tour she consented, and sailed for the United States in December of 1892. Here she was to find a very different public and a very different press from those to which she was accustomed.

Then, as now, the United States ranked publicity as the most important factor in any theatrical enterprise, and this, of all things, Duse despised. She antagonized the newspapers by refusing to give interviews; she could not understand why the public should be interested in her private life or her personal opinions. "From seven to eleven I belong to the public. But for the rest of my time I am a woman like anybody else and have the right to keep my life to myself."

In a letter to her American managers, Carl and Theodor Rosenfeld, she wrote as follows:

"I have always found it possible to succeed in my work without having to resort to methods which are, alas! generally adopted. I intend to adhere to my resolution, even in a country like America, where, I am told, exaggerated advertising is absolutely necessary. I believe there is in the United States a public which is cultured, educated and impartial, and that is the only public which interests me. That public is as tired as I am of all this exaggeration which attempts to deceive it and of which one has not the slightest need in order to form an independent and serious judgment."

When Sarah Bernhardt was held up as a shining example of "cooperation," Duse became even more adamant—her ways were different. To her it was "the work" that mattered, and she refused to jeopardize it by pouring out her much needed vitality on what seemed to her trivial. This mania had not yet reached Europe in those days; there an artist was judged by her performance, not by her personal idiosyncrasies. "Let them come and see my work," Duse said.

But the press refused to understand. The frustrated reporters retaliated by calling Duse "neurotic," "temperamental," "egotistical"; they ridiculed her desire for seclusion and called her "the hermit of Murray Hill."

She opened in January 1893 at the Fifth Avenue Theatre in *La Dame aux Camélias*, to a half-empty house. But the miracle of her acting was recognized by the more discriminating members of her audience, and, while this first American tour (which included Boston and Chicago) was no triumph, she succeeded in winning many friends; among them Richard Watson Gilder—editor of the *Century* magazine—and his wife Helena became especially dear to her. In their home on Clinton Place she found comfort and understanding.

She returned to Italy worn out after eighteen months of incessant travel. It was nearly a year before she was strong enough to act again. Only her most intimate friends knew the real cause of those spells of exhaustion which forced her from time to time to take long periods of rest. She suffered from the same illness which destroyed her mother: tuberculosis. Her doctors marvelled at her ability to survive the severe hemorrhages from which she frequently suffered. It was only her strong will to live that saved her. She never talked about it—it was a well-guarded secret—but there is no doubt that this long-standing weakness of her lungs contributed to the fatal effects of the pneumonia that assailed her in Pittsburgh in 1924.

It was Joseph Schurman who persuaded Duse to play a return engagement in the United States in 1896. He was a shrewd impresario—in the fullest sense of this misused word—and believed, rightly as it turned out, that her first American tour had been mishandled. Under his management, he felt, she would have a great success there. But first he wanted her to appear in London.

When Duse opened at Drury Lane, Sarah Bernhardt had just finished a season at Daly's, and for the first time in her dazzling career *la grande Sarah's* supremacy was challenged. Critics and public were now divided in their allegiance. No less a critic than George Bernard Shaw headed the Duse faction, and proclaimed *her* the greatest living actress. Queen Victoria, wishing to form her own judgment, summoned Duse to play at Windsor Castle. Since Her Majesty demanded "something cheerful," Duse chose *La Locandiera* and the Queen was entranced by her incomparable Mirandolina. Word spread that Her Majesty had been "much amused," and this greatly enhanced Duse's popularity with the British public. The London engagement was a complete success and Schurman was delighted. He felt confident that results in the United States would be equally rewarding.

Though he had no better luck than Tänczer in persuading Duse to "meet the press," he was clever enough to make an asset out of this liability. He played up the aloofness and reserve of Duse's personality, and managed to make her inaccessibility seem mysteriously attractive. Duse found herself received with deep respect—almost with awe—as though she were some royal personage.

Schurman started the tour in Washington, D.C., with a gala performance of *La Dame aux Camélias*, with President Cleveland and the first lady in attendance. Later, a reception was given for Duse at the White House—an unheard-of honour for an actress in those days. Duse-worship became the fashion. The public flocked to see her everywhere she played. The houses were packed, the applause was ecstatic, the notices glowing, and, as he counted up the enormous grosses, Joseph Schurman was content.

Not long before this second American tour Duse had met Gabriele d'Annunzio—for her a fateful meeting and one that was to bring her much suffering.

One evening in Rome, after a performance of *La Dame aux Camélias*, as Duse made her way to her dressing room, a young man flung himself at her feet, kissed the hem of her dress, crying out *"O grande amatrice!"* as he gazed at her with burning eyes. At least, so goes the story—and it could well be true, for this kind of theatricalism was typical of Gabriele d'Annunzio.

At the time, Duse, still under the spell of Marguerite Gautier's death scene, paid little attention to this extravagant young man; but his eyes haunted her, those "metallic" eyes which had hypnotized and seduced so many women.

Later, in Venice—after her return from America —they met again, and she saw much of him. His creative vitality, the dazzling beauty of his verbal images, his delight in his own genius, his overpowering egotism amazed and enthralled her. She, so reserved, so reticent, so unobtrusive, found something boyish and invigorating in this creature so different from herself. It was the attraction of opposites. She fought to keep their relationship on a platonic basis, but to a man like d'Annunzio, with his colossal vanity, this would have been unthinkable. After a few months he became her lover.

Through his book, *Il Fuoco*, d'Annunzio started the legend which has persisted through the years, of an aging actress—La Foscarina-Duse—sick with passion for a young poet—Stelio-d'Annunzio; but, in fact, at the beginning of their love affair Duse was only thirty-seven, and d'Annunzio only five years younger.

It seemed to Duse that at last she had found "her poet"—the man who would raise the Italian drama to the level she had dreamed of.

When, in 1897, she reluctantly consented to face the Paris public, she begged d'Annunzio to allow her to include his recently finished play *La Città Morta* in her repertoire; but he refused, saying he had promised it to Sarah Bernhardt, whom he secretly thought far superior to Duse—and this was only natural, for Sarah and he had much in common; the charlatan in him responded to the glittering theatricality of the great French actress. Duse was disappointed but quietly accepted his decision, and he compromised by dashing off an inferior piece of work, *Sogno d'un Mattino di Primavera*, which Duse immediately put into rehearsal.

Duse was literally afraid of appearing in the French capital—she frankly admitted it herself. The French are notoriously skeptical of foreign artists. They are far more "insular" than the British. Until an artist has been accepted by the Parisian audience and critics, he does not exist. To some extent this is still true today, but at the turn of the century it was indisputable.

For several years the question of Duse's Parisian engagement had been discussed among her friends and admirers, who constantly urged it on her. Dumas fils advised her, instead of playing in Italian, to play in French; she had studied the language and spoke it fluently, though with a strong Italian accent. "If you work hard for a couple of years you will speak it like a native," wrote Dumas, somewhat optimistically. Duse was more realistic. In any case she would never consider playing in any language but her own; she felt the truth—the cohesion—of her performance would be shattered.

At last, after her triumphs in many other countries had made her, next to Bernhardt, the most talked-of actress of her time, it was thought that Paris too might accept an Italian-speaking company; so, in the spring of 1897, her forthcoming appearance at the Théâtre de la Renaissance was announced.

There are several widely different accounts of this Paris engagement. The Renaissance was Sarah Bernhardt's own theatre, and Victor Mapes in his *Duse and the French*[3] claims that Sarah herself invited Duse to

[3] Published in a limited edition by The Dunlap Society of New York, 1898.

play there—thus giving the impression that Duse was her protégée and she the all-powerful, magnanimous artist who, in the generosity of her princely nature, stretched out a helping hand to this foreign actress— talented no doubt, but still in need of patronage.

E. A. Reinhardt, on the other hand, writes as follows: "Schurman had rented the theatre and on exorbitant terms," and Frances Winwar in her book on d'Annunzio and Duse—*Wingless Victory*—states: "Victorien Sardou whose plays Duse had shown all over the world had cunningly helped to obtain Sarah's consent by assuring her that the Italian actress would never succeed in the exacting French capital."

There is probably truth in all these statements.

It is easy to believe that Sarah—always a shrewd business woman—insisted on "exorbitant terms," but it is also possible that she deliberately circulated the impression, through her press agents, of being in effect Duse's chief sponsor. No other actress had ever been mentioned as a possible rival, and to pose as Duse's champion and protector could only reflect great credit on "*la grande Sarah.*"

There is also controversy as to Duse's choice of an opening bill. Miss Winwar writes: "For her opening Duse, with remarkable courage, chose *The Lady of the Camellias.*" Victor Mapes confidently states that Duse intended to open with *Magda*, but was persuaded by the malicious Sarah to choose *The Lady of the*

Camellias instead, Marguerite Gautier always having been considered Sarah's greatest role.

One is inclined to believe this last version; it was not in Duse's nature gratuitously to offend Sarah, especially as her admiration for the older actress was boundless—and always remained so. In her own words: "I consider her an artist of genius. . . . I admire her high intelligence as well, and I am certain that she has a great and sincere spirit. . . ."

The third point on which most commentators disagree is the reaction to this opening performance. Reinhardt speaks of "enormous success," whereas Bertita Harding (in *Age Cannot Wither*) calls it a "near fiasco." Victor Mapes, who seems to have been present, describes Sarah seated in the stage box "going into" (very disturbingly, one gathers!) "ecstasies over the talent of her protégée," and he continues: "As the audience filed out, after giving one final look at Bernhardt, there could be no doubt as to the result of the issue. If someone had triumphed, it was not Duse."

In an article in *Le Théâtre* of 1902, Felix Duquesnel, recalling Duse's first Parisian performance, writes: "The first impression was complex, strange I might almost say, a defeat of all the customary conventions. One looked in vain for the traditional ideal. . . . One had to grow accustomed to it. One had to overcome prejudice and submit to an initiation."

I believe this last impression is the correct one.

Wherever Duse appeared for the first time this pattern was repeated: the puzzled surprise, the totally new experience which could not be immediately absorbed. It took the public, and particularly the critics, a little time to adjust to this new adventure in the art of acting. Where Bernhardt was "an army with banners" instantly perceptible and triumphantly sweeping all before it, Duse was the "still small voice" which gradually, but all the more powerfully, undermined all resistance, and at last penetrated to the very heart of her audience.

In spite of Sarah's machinations and the initial resistance of the critics, the cumulative impact of Duse's playing finally swept over Paris like a tidal wave, and her triumph was complete. Sarah never forgave *"cette rosse,"* as she called her, and continued all her life to ridicule and minimize her art.

Duse's one disappointment in the Paris engagement was the failure of d'Annunzio's *Sogno d'un Mattino di Primavera*. Her faith in his genius blinded her at this time to the fact that though a great poet he was no playwright. His *Città Morta* had been sold to Sarah Bernhardt, who produced it in Paris as *La Ville Morte* (her actors nicknamed it *La Ville à Mourir*) in 1898, and scored one of her rare failures.

Duse gave herself no rest. She dreamed of creating a theatre in Italy—a sort of Italian Bayreuth—devoted to d'Annunzio's work. For this she needed money, and she made extensive tours throughout Europe and South America, adding to her existing repertoire two new dramas by d'Annunzio : *La Gioconda* and *Francesca da Rimini;* and, since Sarah had not succeeded with *La Città Morta,* d'Annunzio now graciously consented to let Duse play that too.

But in spite of all her efforts his plays were not successful. In Italy they were received with angry shouts and catcalls; and though people everywhere crowded the theatres to see her play, they felt her genius was wasted on these elaborate, verbose tragedies. After the publication of *Il Fuoco,* in which, with execrable taste, d'Annunzio exploited his love affair with Duse, public resentment against him grew so violent that Schurman refused to continue as her manager unless she withdrew the d'Annunzio plays from her repertoire. This Duse refused to do.

Through George Tyler an American tour was arranged for the fall of 1902. I have in my possession a series of letters from Tyler to Duse's representative, a Mr. Joseph Smith, in which the American attitude towards d'Annunzio is clearly expressed. During the preliminary negotiations for the tour, in 1901, Tyler writes:

"Dear Mr. Smith, I have your letter and note what you say in reference to the Duse-D'Annunzio combination—I cannot say that I think well of the proposition—Madame Duse can come to America and play a most successful season—if Mr. D'Annunzio accompanies her the results will be disastrous—the reason should be most plain to you. Mr. D's actions towards the lady are very well known in America—His recent book in which the great Italian actress figured as the central character has been thoroughly discussed by the American press with the result that he has gained the contempt of every woman in the land—It is a serious question if Mr. D'Annunzio escape being hissed off the stage —He would not only be a failure himself but he would absolutely ruin her position in America. No, I do not care to consider such a proposition. My offer to Madame Duse still holds good. She does not need a new play—Let her come to us and play her old repertoire—I can assure her the largest season she has ever enjoyed. . . ."

At d'Annunzio's instigation Duse evidently tried to arrange a lecture tour for him as a condition for her own appearances under George Tyler's management, for Tyler, in another letter to Joseph Smith, writes as follows:

"I regret very much that Signor D'Annunzio has such a high estimate of his drawing power. Frankly, between you and I, I believe a lecture tour by this gentleman would be anything but a success. The American people dont care to hear anyone lecture in French or Italian. There would only be one out of every hundred in the audience who would know what he was talking about. Furthermore, I dont think there would be over a hundred in any audience. . . . I can only suggest that you use every means in your power to dissuade him from attempting the lecture tour. It really seems outrageous that Signora Duse, who could come to America and do perhaps the biggest business ever done by a foreign artist, has to be hampered by this proposition. . . . I dont believe she will ever come if she insists upon the condition that his lecture tour must be arranged."

And in a subsequent letter to Mr. Smith, dated November 9th, 1901, Tyler firmly reiterates his objections:

"If I am forced to lose Madame Duse I shall regret it very much indeed, but I dont propose to lose a whole lot of money on D'Annunzio with the full knowledge that his coming is a hindrance instead of a help. She will be a success whether he comes or not, and oh so much greater success if he stays at home. Furthermore it would be so much better, if he does come, to come modestly and quietly and travel along as excess baggage without making any fuss about it. . . . Let him come if he will, but not to talk. I wonder if it ever occurs to D'Annunzio that he would be doing the lady inestimable harm by this arrangement."

The idea that d'Annunzio could ever "travel along as excess baggage" is highly comical—and since modesty and quietness were simply not in his nature, the idea of his accompanying Duse was abandoned. Unfortunately, however, she insisted on limiting her repertoire to d'Annunzio's plays and, due to this, the season was a failure, so he was "a hindrance instead of a help" after all.

Duse was never able to convince the public, or the critics, of d'Annunzio's genius as a playwright, and her loyal efforts ended in personal disillusionment and financial disaster, particularly since she had lavishly poured her own money into these productions.

She was forced to return to her old repertoire, and played a highly successful season in London in 1903.

Meanwhile d'Annunzio had written a new tragedy, *La Figlia di Iorio;* he had promised the play to Duse and she had agreed to appear in it in Milan with the Virgilio Talli Company. She worked on it as she had never worked on any play before. Then, suddenly, she fell ill, and d'Annunzio, refusing to postpone the opening, gave her part to Irma Grammatica. This betrayal Duse could not forgive. She had forgiven him his countless affairs with other women, she had forgiven him his book *Il Fuoco,* which he had published against her wishes; as a woman she was ready to forgive him almost anything, but this was an affront to her as an artist, and, as an artist, she at last rebelled.

Ironically, *The Daughter of Iorio* was the only play of d'Annunzio's that achieved success.

In 1904 Duse met the French director Lugné-Poë —creator of the famous Théâtre de L'Oeuvre in Paris —and his wife, the talented young actress Suzanne Déсprès. L'Oeuvre was what we would call today an "avant-garde" theatre; it had introduced many foreign playwrights to the Parisian public, including Ibsen and Maeterlinck, and Duse followed its work with passionate interest. During the rehearsals of Gorki's *Lower Depths*, Duse gave Lugné-Poë many valuable suggestions. L'Oeuvre was always struggling against financial difficulties—that seems to be the usual pattern of such theatres, then as now—and Duse suggested that she should play Vasilissa with the company for a final gala performance. Lugné-Poë in his book *Sous les Etoiles* writes: "I asked her what her salary would be. 'What do you pay the boy who's so good as the lunatic?' she asked. 'Ten francs,' I answered. 'Then pay me that,' she said."

True to her rule Duse acted in Italian, while the others played in French. The event was received with such enthusiasm that the deficit was temporarily wiped out, and the work at L'Oeuvre was able to continue.

This was the beginning of Duse's association and friendship with Lugné-Poë. He replaced Schurman as her manager, and arranged engagements for her all over Europe—in Italy, Germany, Austria, Hungary, Rumania, Holland, Belgium, France, England and Scandinavia. Maeterlinck's *Monna Vanna* was added to her repertoire, and three plays by Ibsen—"Ibsen my saviour," as she called him—*Hedda Gabler*, *Rosmersholm* and *The Lady from the Sea*.

In June of 1907 she embarked on a tour of South America—then Europe again: four long years of incessant touring, of unremitting work.

Then, in 1909, she suddenly decided to leave the stage.

Lugné-Poë claims she frequently threatened to do this. In his book *Sous les Etoiles* he writes: "She would often announce to me her decision to stop working, to give up the stage; as proof that her decision was irrevocable she spoke of cancelled contracts, of plays refused and returned, etc. . . . But I guessed that I was not supposed for one moment to admit this possibility—it was only a test; if I had admitted it, she would have been furious, and turned the full force of her fury on me."

This time, however, her decision *was* irrevocable, and after a performance of *The Lady from the Sea* in Berlin, she disbanded her company for good.

Duse was only fifty-one when she gave up the theatre. No one understood her reasons. The popular explanation was that she was "crushed by d'Annunzio's desertion"—but this was manifestly untrue, since she broke finally with him in 1904, and in the following five years had worked continuously. Like the great artist she was, she translated suffering into beauty and, from all accounts, played more superbly than ever before.

People never believe in the possibility of an actor really *wanting* to leave the stage—yet it can happen. The fact that Duse was the supreme actress of her time only made it the more incredible. It was not despair, not personal sorrow, certainly not failure that made her leave the theatre. It might perhaps be called "disenchantment." She realized her dream of an ideal theatre would never be fulfilled, or at least that she herself would never be able to fulfill it.

During one of our talks in 1923 Duse told me she felt she had "failed." This, of course, seemed to me fantastic; yet, young as I was, I dimly understood her meaning. "The supreme misfortune is when theory outstrips performance," Leonardo wrote. Duse's vision of the theatre had been so high that, according to her own standards, she had failed it.

Many artists, as they grow older, feel this sense of disillusionment—of disenchantment. In his last years, at the height of his fame, Ibsen wrote: "There is, of course, a certain satisfaction in becoming so well-known in these different countries. But it gives me no sense of happiness. And what is it really worth—the whole thing?"

So Duse felt, at the height of her fame in 1909:
"What is it really worth?" The theatre was no longer
enough for her. She felt she must find the "state of
grace" outside it, beyond it, within herself. In this,
the turbulence of theatre life could only be a hindrance, so she turned her back on it, and spent the
next twelve years groping, searching, growing toward
that state of grace. When she was forced to act again
in 1921, those in her audience with eyes to see felt
that she had surely found it.

Duse's daughter, Enrichetta, had married a young
Englishman, a professor at Cambridge University. On
hearing of her mother's retirement, she begged her to
come and share her life with them. But Duse was afraid
of the effect her presence might have on her daughter's
happiness. She had seen her through the years as often
as her work permitted, had watched over her from afar,
and amply provided for her well-being and education.
She had never wanted her to become involved in the
turmoil of stage life and, indeed, it was not until she
was grown-up that the child knew of her mother's
fame. They were temperamentally very different, and
though Duse loved her dearly, she knew it would be
unwise for them to try and live together. Also, Enrichetta and her husband were both ardent Catholics,
both belonging to the Third Order of St. Dominic, and
Duse was aware that she could never travel the same

road in her search for spiritual development. She had always known this. In her own words:

"Dès que l'intransigeance de la doctrine et l'aspect purement écclésiastique entrent en jeu, je suis rebelle."[4]

She was convinced that she must pursue her pilgrimage alone.

At first she made her home in Florence, then moved to a house near Rome. Her friend the German banker Robert von Mendelssohn had taken charge of her savings, and the investments he made for her assured her of a steady, though modest, income. She moved restlessly from place to place; after so many years of incessant travel it was hard to settle down; the roving spirit of her seafaring ancestors was strong within her. But, at last, she found an old house in Asolo—a small hill-town not far from her beloved Venice. She wrote to the playwright Marco Praga: "This is where I should like to spend my last years, and this is where I should like to be buried. Remember that, and when the time comes, let it be known. . . ."

Then, in 1914, came the war.

Duse was possessed by a desire to serve, to alleviate in some small way the terrible suffering she saw all about her. Once more she started travelling—visiting hospitals throughout Italy, giving courage to the

---

[4] . . . As soon as doctrinal intransigence and a purely ecclesiastical point of view enter in, I rebel.

wounded, writing letters for them, running errands for them. She poured out her strength, and what money she could lay her hands on, to bring them comfort. But what they remembered most in later years was her shining spirit, the healing grace of her wonderful hands, her profound and simple understanding of their torment; they felt that she actually shared it with them—and this was true.

She went back to Asolo when the war ended, to find herself penniless. Her savings had vanished with the collapse of the German mark.

She returned to the theatre as she had started out in it—through sheer necessity.

Without financial resources she did not dare engage actors of her own, but her old friend and comrade Zacconi suggested her playing with his company, and she gratefully accepted.

She opened in Rome in May 1921 with Ibsen's *The Lady from the Sea*, followed a few days later by Marco Praga's *La Porta Chiusa*. She was received with wild enthusiasm. Those who had known her work before her retirement sensed an extraordinary change in her. It was not only that she looked older—far older than her years—but they felt in her a new, mysterious power. In the *Corriere della Sera*, Renato Simoni wrote: "From act to act we saw her rising to greater heights, yet the greatness of her presentation was veiled by the stark simplicity of her speech . . . every word revealed a mystery to us."

To those who saw her for the first time, her acting was a miracle.

Less than a month later she repeated her success in Milan. All Italy rejoiced in the return of their "incomparable Duse."

She was filled with humility and gratitude by the extraordinary response of her audiences. She had felt so old—so unsure. But now, her strength and courage were renewed. Though her lungs suffered from the unaccustomed effort of speaking on the stage, and between performances she was torn by terrible spasms of coughing, she was determined to go on. She was sustained by the knowledge that she was still needed, that she could still "serve"—perhaps better than ever before. Besides, she had discovered a new play by a young Italian author—Gallarati-Scotti—and, after some months of rest, she put it into rehearsal, this time with a company of her own.

The play was *Così Sia*, and the first performance took place in Rome in the fall of 1921. In spite of her personal success, which was as great as ever, she was disappointed in the critical reception of Scotti's work; but she believed in it, and kept it in her repertoire, to which she now added Ibsen's *Ghosts* and a revised version of d'Annunzio's *Città Morta*. With these five plays she toured all over Italy during 1922. Her health made it impossible for her to act regularly every night, but the theatres, for the most part, were rented by the week, and her company had to be paid on a weekly basis too, so, in spite of all the acclaim and adulation, the year ended with a considerable deficit.

It happened that an English lady, Miss Catherine Onslow, saw Duse play several times in Milan and in other cities during this Italian tour. She became one of Duse's most ardent admirers and, having heard of her financial difficulties, she determined to seek her out and see if there was any way in which she could be of help. Miss Onslow had many important connections in London and, on her return there, she was able to raise enough money to settle some of the more pressing obligations and, through her influence, the well-known English theatre-manager, Charles Cochran, became interested in bringing Duse to London.

At the same time Morris Gest, who was in Europe arranging to bring the Moscow Art Theatre and Max Reinhardt's company to America for a fall season, heard of Duse's triumphant return and persuaded her to accept a New York engagement under his management.

Duse opened a series of performances at the Oxford Theatre in London in the summer of 1923, with a repertoire of five plays: Ibsen's *Lady from the Sea* and *Ghosts*, Scotti's *Così Sia*, Praga's *Porta Chiusa*, and d'Annunzio's *La Città Morta*. The large house was completely sold out weeks in advance, tickets were at a premium, and the enthusiasm—both of press and

[63]

public—was overwhelming. Following these performances in London, Duse played several engagements in
Germany and Austria; then, after a short rest, she
embarked for New York in October 1923.

This time America received her with all the reverence due to a supreme artist. Morris Gest was not only
a brilliant impresario, but a true lover of the theatre—
the two do not necessarily go together!—and he was
fortunate in having as his financial backer the well-
known patron of the arts Otto H. Kahn, who also happened to be a rare and understanding human being.
Together they protected Eleonora Duse, guarded her
privacy, and made sure she had the peace so necessary
to her physical and spiritual well-being.

She opened on Monday evening, October 29th, at
the Metropolitan Opera House in *The Lady from the
Sea*. The next day *The New York Times* reported as
follows: "Every seat and all the standing-room at the
Metropolitan Opera House was filled last night by the
crowd that went to see Eleonora Duse in her first appearance on the American stage for twenty years. People stood three and four deep in the space at the rear
of the orchestra seats. . . . More than one-hundred-
and-fifty extra seats in the musician's pit helped take
care of the crowd.

"The box-office for general-admission tickets did
not open until 7:30 P.M. but a line began to form in
front of the window at 8 o'clock in the morning. The

line grew in length until it wound past the front of the Opera House on Broadway, through 39th St. and Seventh Avenue and almost entirely around the building. When the ticket window opened, every one of the general-admission tickets was sold in ten minutes and hundreds of disappointed drama lovers were left outside. They waited patiently until after the curtain went up before they began to drift away.

"Morris Gest announced that the sale of tickets brought in more than $30,000 'The largest receipts in history for a regular dramatic performance. ' . . . At the end of the performance Madame Duse received a remarkable ovation. She was called before the curtain again and again. The audience surged toward the stage, and many tried to speak to her."

This pattern was repeated whenever and wherever she played on this final tour.

Her other performances in New York City, all matinees, took place at the Century Theatre on 62nd Street and Central Park West—the vast auditorium built in 1909 to house the ill-fated New Theatre Company, nicknamed "the Millionaires' Theatre." She played on Tuesday and Friday afternoons. The first Friday *The Lady from the Sea* was repeated, then followed two performances each week of the other four plays in her repertoire.

Since I was playing in *The Swan* at that time, I was unable to attend the Metropolitan Opera House opening, but I had the great good fortune of seeing all nine matinees at the Century, from a seat on the first row, which I had secured weeks ahead from the Morris Gest office.

Duse's contract with Morris Gest called for twenty performances: ten in New York City and the rest divided between Baltimore, Philadelphia, Washington and Boston. She received $2,500 a performance—which amounted to $5,000 a week, from which she had to pay her own expenses and those of her large company, as well as their salaries. In Italy this had seemed a very handsome sum, but the unexpectedly high cost of living in America reduced her actual profit to a minimum. So when Fortuno Gallo offered her more generous terms for an extension of her tour, she gladly accepted.

Under Gallo's management she went south to New Orleans, and then to Havana, Cuba. Back in the United States she played Los Angeles and San Francisco. In spite of the fatigue of constant travel, her health bore up pretty well in these cities where she found warmth and sunshine; but in the last week of March the tour led toward the cities of the Middle West, as yet scarcely touched by spring.

In *Sous les Etoiles* Lugné-Poë makes this strange assertion: "Duse left sunny California, where her stay had been enchanting, on a *sudden caprice*. She broke off her engagement there and *insisted* on returning to

New York via Pittsburgh." And a couple of pages further on he adds another astounding statement: "She desired and *demanded* these long train-trips in North America, comprising journeys three or four days in length." (The italics are mine.)

Lugné-Poë couldn't have been more mistaken! Désirée Wertheimstein, who had been Duse's companion for nearly thirty years, told me herself of Duse's anguish at leaving California, of her dread of the cold weather in the East, and of her horror at the thought of facing Pittsburgh—"*la plus hideuse ville du monde,*"[5] as she called it.

Duse had nothing to do with the itinerary of the tour; the bookings would necessarily have had to be made well in advance, so there could have been no question of her playing Pittsburgh on a "sudden caprice." Mr. Lugné-Poë is obviously ignorant of the way such a tour is managed in "North America."

On April 5th, 1924, Duse played in Pittsburgh at the huge Mosque Auditorium.

Désirée described to me what happened on that day. Her account differs widely from that given by Lugné-Poë; but since she was actually present, I prefer to take her word for it.

Duse was staying at the Schenley Hotel, close to the Auditorium, which could be seen from the windows of her room. Though it was raining—an icy rain, half

[5] The most hideous town in the world.

sleet—she insisted on walking to the theatre, against Désirée's objections.

How well one knows those vast, cold buildings; a solid block of closed doors, all alike, all firmly locked but one—which one searches for in vain.

The two women pounded on one door after another, but there was no response. The front entrance to the Auditorium was not yet open, as there were still two hours before the performance was due to start— Duse always arrived at the theatre far ahead of time. The stage door—in no way different from the rest— was on the far side of the building, and by the time they at last discovered it they were both drenched, and Duse was chilled through and through. She sat shivering in front of an electric heater in her portable dressing room—a tiny oasis of warmth on that huge drafty stage. Désirée insisted on her swallowing some brandy, rubbed her down with alcohol, and wrapped her in the thick blue woolen robe she always wore backstage.

That afternoon in Pittsburgh forty-five hundred people saw Duse play with a magical power, a spiritual intensity which even Désirée had never seen in her before. It was her last performance. The play was *La Porta Chiusa*—"The Closed Door."

Pneumonia developed. In those days there were no "wonder drugs," and for two weeks Duse, attended by two doctors, battled for her life.

I spoke to one of the doctors by telephone on the night of April 20th. He said there was still hope, and seemed to feel the crisis had been passed. But early the next morning her strength gave out, and she died in Désirée's arms. Her last words were:

"Pack the trunks. We must move on!"

It was April 21st, 1924.

Her body was taken back to Italy and she was buried, according to her wish, in the little cemetery in Asolo. Her beloved Monte Grappa stands guard over her grave. A plain slab of white marble covers it, with the simple inscription:

ELEONORA DUSE

1858–1924

IV

ON READING THE MEMOIRS OF PEOPLE WHO knew Duse—or thought they knew her—at various periods of her life, one is struck by the extraordinary discrepancy in their impressions of her. Some speak of her as though she were all goodness, all tenderness—above all, all sadness; a sort of Mater Dolorosa. Others write of her cruelty, her intolerance, her monumental selfishness. There are descriptions, too, in contrast to the "tragic" legend which grew up around her, of her infectious gaiety, her childlike sense of fun and mischief.

According to some, she was a solemn, dedicated "high priestess" of the art of the theatre; one who suffered without ceasing and immolated herself on the altar of her art. Then, again, one reads of her loathing of the theatre, her contempt for her fellow-players. Gordon Craig, in his magazine *The Mask*, refers several times to her statement: "To save the theatre the theatre must be destroyed, the actors and actresses must all die of the plague: they poison the air, they make art impossible"—a statement that has become famous. I remember Duse saying to me once—in a moment of exasperation at her leading man, who had just made a big scene about the location of his dressing room—*"acteur est synonyme d'imbécile!"*[1]—but it would never occur to me to proclaim this as her considered opinion of her colleagues.

I certainly would not have the temerity to say I knew Duse well, but I knew her well enough to know that no one person could ever have known all of her— she was so many different people. This is true of most people to some extent, but in her case it was particularly striking. Added to the myriad facets of her own nature were those of the many women she brought to life on the stage—characters ranging from the gay, sly, enchanting Mirandolina in *La Locandiera*, to the poisonous woman in *La Femme de Claude*. Every great actor must, almost of necessity, be a highly complex creature: potentially both demon and saint, with countless delicate degrees of good and evil jostling and overlapping between the two. And Duse was the greatest actress of her time—perhaps of all time.

Arthur Symons wrote of Duse: "She is the artist of her own soul," and he was right. She had much to combat. When she was very young, the extreme hard-

[1] Actor is synonymous with imbecile.

ship of her life, the bitter loneliness of her struggle, forced her into a sobriety beyond her years. She was shy, inhibited, overly serious. Until she met Cafiero she had lived under a strict, almost monastic discipline. The awakening to ecstasy, the sudden glimpse of pleasures, luxuries and extravagances of which she had never even dreamed, revealed traits in her nature which, for many years, were to dominate her way of life. As success came to her, she was increasingly able to indulge her passion for beautiful surroundings, beautiful things, beautiful people. She became extravagant not only in material ways, but in behaviour and temperament. There no longer seemed to be any need for discipline.

In her work it was different; in that she was always severe with herself—almost harsh. But as a woman she made no effort to control her whims, her wildly fluctuating moods, her almost pagan sensuality.

She was blessed—one might also call it cursed—with a power of magic so strong that, when she chose to use it, no creature could escape from it. It was, of course, this same "magic" that cast such a spell over her audience. It was not "sex-appeal" but something infinitely more subtle, more dangerous and more complex. Lugné-Poë says: "Her power of attraction was unimaginable, for the very reason, perhaps, that it was satanic." Those who succumbed to it were bound to her forever, no matter how cruelly she might have

wounded them. Tebaldo Checchi, for instance, thought
of her as he lay dying, and left all he possessed to her
and their daughter Enrichetta; this was in 1920,
thirty-four years after their separation. Matilde Serao
writes: "One of the last times Eleonora came to see me,
she murmured suddenly after sitting down in her
chair: 'Poor Tebaldo—would you believe it, Matilde,
that he left a legacy for Enrichetta and me? He left it
to us—think of that. He had laid by a few savings—
a few thousand lire—and they came to us just when we
needed them—always the same Tebaldo.' "

In reading the various accounts it is, of course,
necessary to consider the stages in Duse's life to which
they refer. The two accounts I have found most interesting and revealing are those written by Lugné-Poë,
who was closely associated with her as her manager
between 1904 and 1908, and by Edouard Schneider,
who did not meet her until 1921 when she returned to
the stage. One would think they had been written about
two entirely different women.

Lugné-Poë prefaces his remarks by saying: "Very
few people really knew Eleonora Duse who met the
actress. And those who did know this extraordinary
woman intimately have remained silent, either out of
nobility of spirit, out of discretion, or simply through
fear of being considered sacrilegious, ungrateful icon-
oclasts."

No one, reading his book, could accuse Lugné-Poë

of discretion. In spite of his obvious adoration of her—for he was certainly under the spell of her "satanic" attraction—he manages to create a terrifying picture of a spoiled, capricious "diva"—one who, he claims, gave her greatest performances *off* the stage, and who lived a life of the utmost "theatricality." He seems to have felt a kind of love-hate emotion for her as a woman.

His admiration for her as an artist was boundless. In describing the first time he saw her act, he writes: "All that I had hoped from it [the theatre], all that I had believed it could be, but which no other actor had ever given me—so that I had almost begun to doubt its possibility—I found that evening. I knew then that I had been right. . . . My adoration for the theatre was renewed . . . and I adored this woman who had so magnificently revealed it to me."

But some of his remarks about her private life are so exaggerated and so vicious, one is tempted to think there was a good deal of envy mixed up in his feeling for her—the envy of an inferior artist with an inflated ego, for one so infinitely superior.

Her favorite author, he claims, was Machiavelli—whose works she knew "by heart" and whose precepts she studiously adopted. She was devious, hypocritical, domineering, arrogant; given to all kinds of malicious tricks and subterfuges. She used people—even her closest friends—mercilessly, to feed her own insatiable ego. "She pried into their most secret lives, exploited them, discussed them, fictionalized them, sullied them if need be, dramatized them. . . . Couples would leave her presence hopelessly confused, divided—sometimes forever. This was theatre! . . . She was well aware of the suffering she caused by her calculated cruelty; she delighted in pitting one friend against another by rousing suspicion, unleashing anger. . . . She needed to do this, and was unable to give a performance without this stimulus."

In describing the beginning of what he calls a "normal" day, Lugné-Poë tells us that Duse's secretary had orders to report at seven in the morning, bringing her all the newspapers. Even at that early hour he was obliged to appear in evening clothes. She went through every paper, avidly reading every word that was written about her—even in the gossip columns. At 8 :30 her maid appeared and, from then on, all through the day, her *"état-major"*—her general staff—had to be on call. "No one dared to leave; they had to wait around until dismissed." They lived in terror of her moods; they were perennially exhausted. This frightening woman seemingly possessed the devil's own vitality. Lugné-Poë appears to believe that Duse's physical weakness was mainly a pretense, and that she frequently cancelled performances through sheer caprice. Then he, as her manager, was obliged to make appropriate excuses: "The Signora has a fever; impossible for her to play tonight—perhaps tomorrow." If a doctor was sent for—"they are all donkeys!" she would exclaim, and refuse to see him.

Yet in spite of all the anguish he went through— and he makes much of it!—Lugné-Poë claims to have worshipped her, and talks at great length of the sacrifices he made to serve her.

Wedged in between the many horrifying episodes which he recounts with unsparing detail, there are some enchanting glimpses of other, more agreeable, facets of Duse's nature. He writes of her humour: "This extraordinary creature was often hilarious, sprightly, witty, joyous," and, as an example, he tells of an evening when he and some of her other friends went to the theatre with her in Paris to see a well-known actress play. Duse turned to them and muttered "Hm! You're imitating Madame Duse, wretch!" Then, a few seconds later: "Hm! . . . You're imitating Madame Sarah Bernhardt. . . . Make up your mind! . . . Make up your mind, wretch!" And she laughed like a child.

He speaks of the generous enthusiasm with which Duse helped Suzanne Désprès act Nora in *A Doll's House*, a part which she had so often played herself; and tells of her sending Désprès her Nora costume, with a note full of valuable suggestions, and warm encouragement, ending with the words: "These are truths I have searched for with my heart, for I love you tenderly. Eleonora."

His description of Duse's pilgrimage to Oslo in the hope of seeing Ibsen, in February of 1906, is very moving: "She longed to meet him, to be near him— even for a few seconds. . . . It was an almost sacred desire on her part . . . it haunted her." He tells of her bitter disappointment at discovering that Ibsen was too ill to see anyone, or even to receive a message, and he goes on: "The next morning around noon, Duse and I went and stood opposite Ibsen's house. She had bought a pair of Norwegian boots, for she insisted on going there on foot. . . . We stood facing the corner window through which, it was said, Doctor Ibsen could sometimes be seen, attended by his nurse or secretary. In spite of the cold, in spite of the harsh light, Duse waited. . . . On the pavement, opposite his dwelling, Eleonora Duse kept watch, hoping for a glimpse of the old poet." There is not much arrogance in that! It sounds more like humility. Then Lugné-Poë sums up Duse's grief at failing to meet Ibsen by one of his typical overdramatizations: "Eleonora Duse's life stopped there." And the phrase is in italics!

It is this kind of exaggeration, together with certain factual inaccuracies, such as those pointed out earlier in connection with her last American tour, which makes many of his statements suspect. It was perhaps Lugné-Poë's own "theatricality" which made him ascribe "theatricality" to Duse; and possibly his own colossal egotism—which emerges so clearly in his writing—contributed to the warped image he projects of her. There might also have been something in his personality which aroused the perversity in hers. He strikes one as a nervous, neurotic, slightly hysterical man; he admits to being in deadly fear of her, and his behaviour toward her was never natural or relaxed. This, alone, would have been enough to stir the demon in her. And since, judging from his book, he lacked humour and she did not, she might have been tempted to make a gull of him and give him the kind of performance he anticipated. In any case, nothing else I have ever read about her, been told about her, or observed in her myself, gave an impression of either "theatricality" or deviousness.

Perhaps it is a case of a biography revealing the biographer even more than it reveals the biographee.

In turning to Edouard Schneider's book on Duse, we meet a totally different human being. And perhaps after twelve years she really *was* totally different. Perhaps she could have said, with the Mohammedan Bayazid: "For twelve years I was the smith of my own soul. I put it in the furnace of austerity and burned it in the fire of combat, I laid it on the anvil of reproach and smote it with the hammer of blame until I made of

my soul a mirror. Five years I was the mirror of myself and was ever polishing that mirror with divers acts
of worship and piety. Then for a year I gazed in contemplation. On my waist I saw a girdle of pride and
vanity and self-conceit and reliance on devotion and
approbation of my works. I laboured for five years
more until that girdle became worn out and I professed Islam anew. I looked and saw that all created
things were dead. I pronounced four *akbirs* over them
and returned from the funeral of them all, and without intrusion of creatures, through God's help alone,
I attained unto God."

Schneider dedicates his book: "To the sainted
memory of Eleonora Duse, to those faithful ones who
understood and loved her, to her unknown friends that
they too may know her and venerate her."

This dedication sets the tone of the whole book.

"Truth, action, work; let us never forget these
three words, for they illuminate Duse's long struggle,"
Schneider writes. He comments on the total misunder-
standing of her nature, even by people who were supposed to love her: "How often have I heard them
mutter, 'She is terrifying, she is mad!' More than one
of her former colleagues, even during the periods
when she was away from the stage, allowed themselves
to speak of her with bitter malevolence, as though of-
fended by the memory of her greatness. . . . Poor
critics imprisoned in their own mediocrity. They re-

mind one of Renan's cruel words: 'The vulgarity of mankind imposes spiritual solitude on those who, by their genius or greatness of heart, transcend them.' "

Schneider by no means minimizes Duse's difficult, mercurial nature; he admits it fully: "She was changeable as the sea," he says; but the fact that she faced it, deplored it, throughout her life fought to control it, and, at last to a great extent overcame it, he finds wholly admirable.

One of her friends said to her once: "How well I understand the struggle in you between the artist and the woman"; and Duse replied: "The woman, the woman! Don't you know that there are a thousand women in me, and that I am tormented by each one in turn?"

She knew herself better than anyone else ever knew her.

Schneider had seen her play during her first Paris engagement in 1897. Overcome by the power of her genius, like most people he found it incomprehensible when she retired in 1909 at the height of her fame; and when, in 1912, he finished a play which he thought might interest her, he sent it to her, and received a gracious letter, full of appreciation for his work, but nevertheless refusing it.

Then, in 1921, he was present at her first performance in Milan after her long absence from the

theatre, and it was then that he met her; subsequently
he and his wife became very close to her. He writes of
this first meeting: "Not one word, not one inflexion,
not one gesture, revealed a woman of the stage." Her
simplicity and humility amazed him, and the deep
respect he felt for her developed into an ardent and
steadfast devotion.

He had another play in mind and outlined it to
her at this time. She became enthusiastic over the idea
and begged him to set to work on it. He speaks of her
extraordinary capacity to inspire others: "She made
one feel capable of overcoming all obstacles . . ."; of
her passion for work: "Work, that's the only remedy,"
she would say. "One must go on, go on till one can go
no further—and even beyond that!"

He tells of Duse's feeling that the theatre should
be an instrument for good—for service. Her dream
was to have a small theatre of her own: "Quite small,
quite simple, with plain white-washed walls—no orna-
ments. Very little scenery. The things that matter are
that one should be heard clearly, and be able to create
a genuine communion between audience and player."
There she wanted to present plays of high spiritual
value—to experiment, to innovate; to clear the theatre
of all commercial clutter: "Chase the money-changers
from the temple!"

She detested anything rigid, anything to do with

dogma or scholasticism. "Precepts, conventions—above all traditions—have no value in art. . . . Anyone who presumes to *teach* art has no understanding of it."

The year before her return to the stage she was asked by Yvette Guilbert—who knew she was in need of money—to join her in America and start a school of acting there. Duse was amused and said to her friend Madame Casale: "Do you know how I would start my lessons? By telling the students: Don't go to a school!"

When he began work on his new play, Schneider and his wife went to stay at a small inn in Merano, and Duse joined them there. He speaks of her "inexhaustible goodness," her kindness and generosity, her consideration for others, her grace and modesty. "There would be a light tap at the door: 'It's Methuselah!' she would call out gaily. 'May I come in? Are you sure I'm not disturbing you?' and in she would come laughing, young in spite of her white hair and ravaged face, bringing a flower for my wife, a book for me."

Schneider says she was possessed by "a thirst for knowledge." She was a passionate reader. She was interested in everything: "Literature, philosophy, memoirs, travels, religion, social problems, music, painting . . . and on all these subjects her views gave proof of a rare intuition." He quotes her as saying: "I know nothing, nothing! I have everything to learn.

Twelve years ago, when I left the theatre, I did so with
no regrets. I was tired of living for others; I wanted to
live for myself, and learn and learn!"

But now that she was acting again, she was anxious
to find new plays—constructive plays—which might
serve to counteract the weariness and cynicism of post-
war years. Schneider's play, *Exaltation*, appealed to
her strongly; she was eager to produce it, but it was
necessary to find a suitable translator since it was
written in French.

Schneider next saw her in Venice. She had a small
room on the top floor of the Hotel de l'Europe, and
he would find her sitting at her window overlooking
the Grand Canal opposite Santa Maria della Salute, and
watching through field glasses the yachts and cargo
vessels of all sorts sailing in and out of the Giudecca.
She was calm and happy. "You seem to love the sea,"
he said to her. "Love it!" she exclaimed, her eyes
shining; "to me the earth means nothing . . . I am a
child of the sea . . . a daughter of Chioggia!" And
she went on to speak of Ellida in *The Lady from the
Sea*, "My beloved Ellida, so lovely, so alone, so mis-
understood; people thought her mad! . . . When she
tells of olden times when men lived in the sea, and of
how beautiful and free life was then, the others laugh
at her and say, 'Don't listen to her! She's mad!' " And
with flashing eyes she spoke of the Florentine critic
who had dared to call Ellida "hysterical.". . . "Simply

because he never met her in his editorial offices, she had to be 'hysterical.'. . . The imbecile! . . . Why do we always go back to those infernal cities. . . . One should flee from cities!"

It was a little later, when Schneider visited Asolo, that he and Duse for the first time discussed matters of religion and mysticism.

He describes her house—simple, austere, un-cluttered—and her bedroom, on the very top floor, with a splendid view of Monte Grappa. "A wide, low bed—with many books on the table beside it: her faithful, indispensable friends! . . . A few pictures, of Shelley, Beethoven—none of living people—above all none of herself! . . . What spiritual harmony! The silence of a monastic cell in a high convent tower."

Among the books on her table he was surprised to see Maurice Blondel's *L'Action*, "a philosophical work considered extremely difficult, and one which could only be understood by someone with preliminary knowledge in such subjects; how could one not be surprised to find it in the hands of an actress—even one of genius?" Duse said to him: "I read it last winter. And during these past three months, while working in Turin and Milan, it did me a lot of good— brought me much comfort."

Schneider found it hard to admit that she had really been able to understand and utilize this book, but she discussed it in detail, with such penetration and such obvious command of its contents, that he was forced to change his mind.

Another book which for a long time had been a source of strength to her was *The Confessions of St. Augustine*; and, more recently, she had conceived an ardent love for Catherine of Siena. This saint, "whose faith was translated into action—or rather *was* action—roused in Duse a response that was quasi-fraternal."

Schneider realized then that Duse was increasingly concerned with "spiritual liberation, but always in a manner divorced from any specific form. And when her thoughts drew her back to the theatre, from which at that moment she seemed so far removed, it was with the firm resolve of bringing to it a greater purity through the power of these higher forces."

Schneider saw Duse for the last time in Paris; in the interim she had been gravely ill. But she recovered sufficiently to play her engagement in London, which had been a complete triumph, though, as he says, "she didn't speak of it herself; it was always through others that her friends heard about such things." He found her looking older and very frail. A wracking cough tore at her lungs or, as he writes, "her only lung, since for a considerable time, the other one had ceased to function."

Duse spoke with wonder of Catherine Onslow: "She is a simple woman—not at all an intellectual—

but she has the wisdom of the heart. I must speak of what she did for me—this complete stranger—for it is so beautiful!" and she went on to express her gratitude. Then, with bitterness: "My own country would do nothing for me, nothing! Mussolini came to see me—he saw to it that it was in all the papers! He said to me, 'Madame Duse, we will do everything for you!' —I asked him to pay my company during my illness— I asked nothing for myself—I only wanted my actors to be looked after. Well—he did nothing!" She spoke of d'Annunzio—"the Commander of Fiume," she called him. "He wrote a beautiful letter to the papers about me—reviewing all I had done for Italy; things I had long forgotten; things I certainly would never have thought of mentioning myself. He said it was time Italy did something in return. It was a moving, beautiful letter—but that was all! The Commander of Fiume is like that. He thinks a thing, talks about it, writes it down, and once his thought has been expressed in words, once it has been materialized in writing, that's the end of it. That, to him, is action!"

But when Schneider saw her the next day, her bitterness had passed, and she was gay and smiling. He felt that, after all, her great success in London had given her courage; she spoke hopefully of her forthcoming American tour, and outlined plans for work on her return. She had at last found a translator for *Exaltation*, and was determined, somehow, to put it on.

"We shall do good work—you'll see! All shall be well!"

Duse left for the United States shortly after Schneider's last visit with her. One of her friends told him she had received a cable from her about her New York engagement: "Enormous, enormous, enormous consolation."

After Duse's death Schneider received a letter from a member of her company who was also a close friend —in which Lugné-Poë's assertions are once more definitely refuted. Madame Enif Robert tells of Duse's anguish at the thought of leaving San Francisco, and quotes her as saying: "It's so good here by the warm Pacific. . . . Up there it will be cold again. . . . I'm so frightened, so frightened of the cold!" Madame Robert goes on to say that the success in San Francisco was so great it would have been easy to prolong the engagement there, "but the management refused, or was unable, to change the fixed itinerary. And it was with deep regret that Madame Duse left for the 'terrible north.' "

Schneider says Duse was afraid of death—that she rebelled against it in spite of herself; she once exclaimed to him: "How I have loved life! Isn't it shameful to have loved life so much? . . . I wanted to see everything, to understand it all!"

He remembers the tone of her voice in *The Lady from the Sea* as she cried out: "Freedom—and responsibility"; Schneider felt that Duse herself could be summed up in those two words.

Elements from both these books appeared in conversations I have had with people who knew Duse personally. Of these the one who probably knew her best was Désirée von Wertheimstein. She first saw Duse in Vienna in 1896. She was an Austrian woman of good family, and it can have been no easy matter for her to abandon her home, her relatives and friends, to follow Duse and devote her life to serving her. But this she did, and remained with her until her death.

When I first met Madame Duse I paid little attention to Désirée—she was just someone who was there; someone who ran errands for her, waited on her and looked after her. I wasn't sure at first whether she was a friend, a paid companion, or a servant. Whenever Duse sent for me, Désirée would open the door, and after greeting me and taking my coat, would disappear. Duse always saw people she wanted to talk to, alone. I remember on one visit, when Duse came into the room, she put her arm around Désirée's shoulders and said to me: "Poor Désirée! Just think—she has put up with me for twenty-seven years—she is an angel!"

It was not until some time after Duse's death that Désirée talked about her to me. During the days in New York City, when Duse's body lay in St. Joseph's chapel in the Church of St. Vincent Ferrer, Désirée rarely left her side. She guarded her dead, as she had for so many years guarded her living. In any case, she was too overcome with grief to talk about her then. But later, when I went to Asolo to visit Duse's grave, Désirée was staying there at the Albergo dal Sole. I was surprised to find her staying at an inn, instead of at Duse's house. She intimated that she was not welcome there; she told me Duse's daughter, Enrichetta, was living in the house while settling her mother's affairs, and I gathered their relations were anything but friendly.

Désirée seemed completely lost. She had devoted the best years of her life to serving Duse, and now she did not feel free to go inside her house—a house that had been like a home to her ever since Duse had moved into it. People's motives are hard to understand; I was so young at the time that I was too timid to ask questions, or try to fathom the reasons behind the situation. When I suggested to Désirée that I might call on Enrichetta, she strongly urged me not to; I received the impression that Duse's daughter resented anything or anyone connected with the theatre, especially with her mother's part in it—glorious though that had been.

As we walked toward the cemetery, Désirée for the first time talked to me of Duse. She spoke very frankly of her faults; she used the words capricious, willful—even cruel. But she went on to tell of her passionate remorse when she had wounded someone; her hatred of her "demon" and her struggles to gain control of it. She said she was subject to attacks of the blackest melancholy, when for days she was silent, aloof, inverted, enclosed in some indefinable, inexplicable misery—the "smara," the Venetians call it. Then, suddenly, she would be possessed by an equally inexplicable gaiety, an overpowering zest for life, for laughter, for people, for fun, for mischief—like a "merry child." Désirée spoke with disapproval of Duse's abrupt infatuations: she would take a fancy to people, overwhelm them with attentions, gifts, encouragement—captivate them with her charm—and, just as abruptly, turn against them and dismiss them with an almost savage ruthlessness. "Still," she added, "in spite of their unhappiness, not one of them would have wished to forgo the joy of knowing her."

I remember being shocked and resentful at Désirée's frankness; it seemed like a betrayal. She must have felt this, for she turned to me with a quick smile and said: "She would not have been the great human being she was, unless she had had much to overcome. I wanted you to understand this. You yourself experienced her generosity of spirit; you must have sensed her deep humility; but only those who were with her for many years, as I was, knew of her ceaseless efforts to grow, both as a woman and as an artist. I want you to try to imagine—try to realize—the fantastic praise, the extravagant adulation with which she was inundated; the constant temptation to pride and arrogance to which she was subjected. A lesser person would have been totally destroyed by it."

Later, as I looked back on this conversation, I was grateful to Désirée for her honesty. She knew my devotion to Duse—perhaps she wanted to put it to the test. It would have been easier for her to feed me platitudes, evasions, the usual eulogies; instead she honoured me by feeding me the truth. I saw that in thinking of Duse as an inhuman monster of perfection, I had in fact minimized her greatness; young people are inclined to do this to their heroes. Désirée had helped me to grow up.

Many years ago, one night after a performance, Lou Tellegen came to have supper with me. I was then living in a little apartment on the top floor of 10 Fifth Avenue, at the corner of Eighth Street.

I did not know Tellegen well—but we had many mutual friends. He came backstage that evening after the play—*Liliom*, I think it was—and was so gay and charming, and so complimentary about my work, that I asked him to have supper. We sat talking for hours. He had been Sarah Bernhardt's leading man for several years, and I was fascinated by his stories about "*la grande Sarah*"—some of them very amusing, as stories about this extraordinary woman are apt to be. I had seen him in Paris, when I was still a child, play Essex to her Queen Elizabeth. He was not much of an actor, but he was amazingly handsome in a "Greek god" kind of way, and Sarah had made much of him; he was obviously devoted to her.

Then, to my surprise, he told me he had been in Eleonora Duse's company before joining Sarah Bernhardt. It must have been in an exceedingly minor capacity, for Sarah was supposed to have "discovered" him as a very young man—a "beautiful youth"—with no previous experience on the stage. But I listened with interest to what he had to say about Duse; I had not yet seen her play at that time, and knew little about her.

"*Elle n'était pas bonne camarade,*"[2] he kept repeating. Bernhardt frequently gave great parties for her companies, and, though she was fiercely autocratic, she appears to have been a jovial and, on the whole, a benevolent despot. She revelled in all the outward manifestations of triumph, and her whims and caprices were those usually associated with the "great artist" temperament. But Duse? Though she was usually kind and extremely courteous to her actors, she was never "pally" with them. Perhaps it was only to be expected

[2] She was not a good comrade.

that an actor of Tellegen's type—a man who could in all seriousness write a book entitled *Women Have Been Kind to Me*—should find Duse's reserve and aloofness alien and incomprehensible. He could not understand why she should deliberately avoid the demonstrations of the crowds waiting to salute her after a performance. Why she should dislike such marks of public favor as torch-light processions and noisy gatherings, lasting into the small hours, beneath her hotel windows. When I pointed out that she perhaps looked upon these things as an infringement on her privacy, Tellegen dismissed such an attitude as "affectation," unpardonably egotistical and ungrateful—as well as being "bad for business." Did not her success, after all, depend upon the crowd? He would not consider for a moment the possibility of Duse's shyness being genuine. He scoffed at my suggestion that she might really have needed silence and solitude—particularly after a performance. Wasn't she an actress? Then why couldn't she behave like one?

I thought of Arthur Symons' line: "She [Duse] is an actress by being the antithesis of an actress," but I refrained from mentioning it—to Lou Tellegen it would have made no sense, and there are plenty of people in the "profession" who would have agreed with him.

But I laughed to myself after Tellegen had left:

Eleonora Duse was evidently not one of the "women who had been kind" to him!

In 1927, during the summer before Isadora Duncan's death—a death which, in spite of the ghastly shock to those who loved her, seemed in some strange, tragic way, to be fate's blessing—I had several talks with her. During one of these talks she spoke of Eleonora Duse.

Isadora first met Duse in 1906, when she was invited to dance for her at the Mendelssohns' house in Berlin. She had always adored her as an artist, and from then on she adored her as a friend.

In 1907 Duse commissioned Gordon Craig, somewhat rashly as it turned out, to design her a production of Ibsen's *Rosmersholm*. Since Isadora and Craig were living together at that time, she saw a good deal of Duse. In her autobiography she gives an amusing description of this whole episode. Neither Duse nor Craig were what one might call "easy" people, and Isadora had to use all her guile to keep the peace between them. But this was not what Isadora talked about that day in Paris in 1927. She told of a time several years later—in 1911—when she came to know Duse really well. That was the year when Isadora had to face the tragedy which, in her own words, "completely shattered my force and power," and from which she was never able to recover: her two little children were drowned in the Seine when the car they were riding in met with an accident and plunged into the river.

She told me of how she had fled from Paris, and had wandered alone from one country to another, in a desperate attempt to regain her sanity and find the courage to go on living. She found herself in Italy in the vicinity of Viareggio, where Duse was living at the time. Isadora was not aware of this until she received a note from Duse asking her to come to her. Isadora said she had no idea how Duse found out she was there, but she felt that here was the one person who might help her, the one human being she could bear to see. She went to find Duse and stayed with her for several months.

I'll never forget Isadora's face as she told me of Duse's infinite compassion. "In her great wisdom," she said, "she made no effort to console me. She held me in her arms and wept with me. She encouraged me to tell her about Deirdre and Patrick, to describe their looks, the things they said, all their little ways. I no longer felt alone, and for the first time I was able to talk freely and share my grief. It was as though she felt it as deeply as I did."

She went on to speak of the radiance of Duse's presence, the healing warmth that seemed to flow from her; of her simplicity, her honesty, her acute awareness of Isadora's torment and her fear of what the future might hold in store for her unless she could somehow control her exuberant, vulnerable nature. She implored her not to seek personal happiness again, but to pour all of her energies—all of herself—into her work. "I wish I had listened to her," Isadora said.

During those months together, they discussed the possibility of joining forces to try to re-create the theatre of the Greeks, with its marriage of dance and drama. They talked of a production of *The Bacchae*, with Duse as Agavé, and Isadora directing the chorus and dancing Dionysos. They had worked it out in detail, and as Isadora described it to me, I had a clear vision of how glorious it might have been. But, alas, like so many of Isadora's dreams it was never realized, and as she spoke of it I had the feeling that Duse realized it never could be, and only dwelt on it as a means of helping Isadora to temper her grief by focussing her powers once more upon her art.

Gordon Craig has called Isadora "a far greater genius" than Duse. I'm sure Isadora would not have agreed to that; she was too well aware of her weakness as a human being. She felt—rightly, I think—that a great part of Duse's genius lay in the fundamental strength of her nature. The fluctuating moods, the sudden caprices, the unpredictable behaviour so characteristic of her at certain periods of her life, never affected—or only momentarily affected—the basic stability, the innate power of will and spirit which enabled her to overcome betrayal, illness, suffering, and, at last, the "demon" in herself.

This Isadora failed to do—*knew* she had failed to do.

There was a haunting wistfulness in her eyes as she summed up her feeling about Duse: "She was strong. She was the strongest creature I have ever known."

I first met Helen Lohman in New York one night in the Dominican church of St. Vincent Ferrer.

Duse rested there, in her coffin banked with flowers, from the Sunday when her body was brought to New York from Pittsburgh, until the following Thursday, when, after a solemn funeral Mass, she was taken to the Italian steamship *Duilio*, which sailed that afternoon for Naples.

All those nights, and the greater part of the days, I spent beside Duse's coffin.

I was playing at the time—in *The Swan*—and Father Whalen, prior of the Dominican community, very kindly gave me a key to the baptistry, since by the time I got there after my performance, the church was closed. Désirée and Maria, Duse's maid, were always there, and usually two or three members of her company.

The church was very beautiful during those hours between midnight and dawn. There was no harsh electric light to dispel the shadows, only the flickering candles round the bier, and the coloured votive lights grouped before a statue of the Madonna and banked to one side of the altar rail. In the morning the White Sisters from the adjoining Dominican convent glided like serene ghosts along the gallery above the sanctuary, to attend the first Mass of the day.

As I entered the church on Wednesday midnight, I saw more people than usual gathered in the pews beside St. Joseph's chapel, where Duse's body lay. Among them I noticed a woman dressed in black, with a long pale face and graying hair. She sat next to Désirée, whom she seemed to know; her eyes were red with weeping.

On the far side of the church two figures paced up and down the aisle, engaged in animated conversation. They spoke in whispers, but in the silence the sound was penetrating and distracting. The woman glanced in their direction from time to time, and I could see she was disturbed by their behaviour. After a while I got up, crossed over to them, and asked them to be quiet. When I returned, the woman nodded to me and thanked me. She introduced herself as Helen Lohman. When I told her my name she gave me a penetrating, half-apologetic look: "I thought you were one of those people talking over there," she whispered. I felt rather angry at being so misjudged, but said nothing and sat down again. In the morning, as we were all waiting for the service to begin, Helen Lohman came to me and said: "I shall come and see you play. Madame Duse told me I was to go and find you."

I thought no more about it until one evening some time later, when Helen Lohman came backstage to see me after a performance. From then on I saw a good deal of her and, in 1926, when I started the Civic Repertory Theatre, she joined the staff as play-reader and librarian.

She was a strange woman; in some ways I liked her very much, but there were things about her that puzzled and annoyed me. She was almost pathologically secretive and devious, and the forthright, over-candid, Scandinavian half of me rebelled against these traits in her. This somewhat tempered the warmth of our friendship. Still, I was grateful for her criticism and appraisal of my work, about which she was always honest, sometimes to the point of ruthlessness; during those all-important years in my development as an actress, it was invaluable to me. And I also have to thank her for the many interesting memories she shared with me of Eleonora Duse.

In piecing together her story, which was veiled by an almost occult reticence, I gathered Helen Lohman had been struggling through a black period in her life when she first encountered Duse. She had been living in Europe for some years studying the violin;

her teachers and the critics for whom she played proph-esied a fine career ahead. But an injury to her left hand ended these hopes, and she was forced to put away her violin forever. This, coupled with an un-happy love affair, brought her to the verge of a com-plete nervous breakdown.

It was then that she met Duse.

I was never able to determine the exact circum-stances of their meeting, except that it took place in Paris; but it seems that Duse was about to leave for Italy, and insisted on taking Helen with her. She made her stay with her for several months. Helen spoke of her to me with passionate gratitude, profound devotion, and a rather awed reverence. She seemed overcome with amazement that Duse should have bothered to be so good to her. "After all, who was I," she used to say, "that she should have taken the trouble to save my life?"

Helen Lohman had seen Duse play in some of her greatest roles—I remember she particularly men-tioned Marguerite Gautier and Mirandolina—but she never dreamed that she would one day come to know her. This did not occur until after Duse's retirement from the stage. I got the impression that, in fact, Helen came to know her rather well, and that her devotion did not prevent her from seeing her quite clearly.

"She was a creature of mercurial moods," she told

me. "Though she was kindness itself to me, she would sometimes shut herself in and refuse to talk to me, or even see me, for several days. Then, suddenly she would tap on my door in the middle of the night: 'I'm hungry! Come down to the kitchen with me, Elena, and eat, and have a glass of wine!' Then we would go down and raid the larder and sit at the kitchen table, and she would talk and talk—till dawn. I remember one of those nights she spoke of Ibsen's *The Master Builder*—'my favorite play in all the world,' she called it. She told me she would have given anything to play Hilde Wangel—'but she is not for me,' she said, 'I was not right for her.' And then, there in the kitchen, she *did* play Hilde—with all the youth, the fun, the vitality, the rapacity, of that trold-like creature. It was an extraordinary performance—I sat there spellbound. And suddenly it was morning. She looked at me in bewilderment and laughing like a child exclaimed: 'See how bad I am, Elena! I've kept you up all night. Now you must sleep—you must sleep! Forgive me!' Imagine her asking me to forgive her for giving me such a rare experience!"

"Another night she began talking about *Macbeth*," Helen told me. "She always kept a copy with her, though she could only read a very little English. She knew it in a French translation—but she loved to hear the sound of Shakespeare's own words, and would ask me to read it aloud to her. Then she would sit awhile pondering over it in silence. 'The sound reflects the meaning,' she would say; 'blood; drowsy; incarnadine; those words *sound* like their meaning.' Then, after a moment, she added: 'Of course it is Macbeth himself one would want to play. What an extraordinary, complex nature! In spite of his maleness—so much *woman* in him! Ah, Shakespeare! He knew everything!' "

"She never stopped studying," Helen said. "She was always reading. She would go out in the morning, carrying a rug and a pile of books, stretch out under the trees, a pair of enormous tortoise-shell glasses on her nose, and spend the whole day there—reading, reading, always reading."

When she was at home, in one or the other of her retreats, she gave no thought to her appearance. She wore any old dress, no make-up—she never even looked at a mirror—just brushed her hair straight back and pinned it in a loose knot at her neck. Then, abruptly, she would decide to be "a lady" for a while; a car and chauffeur were sent for, and off she would go to Rome or Paris to visit some of her "grand" friends. On these occasions she would wear the lovely clothes designed for her by Worth, her hair would be exquisitely arranged, and she might even consent to put on a little powder. She used to say, *"Je suis belle quand je veux"* (I am beautiful when I choose). Now and then Helen would accompany her on these expeditions, but more often Duse would go alone. Her return was as sudden and unexpected as her departure; she would cry: "Ah, people, people! They exhaust one! Now I must be alone!" and another period of reading, study and contemplation would begin.

Once, in one of her gay moods, Helen told me, she decided to give a party. Friends in the vicinity were of course invited, but many who lived quite far away were summoned by urgent telegrams. When the day came and the guests started to arrive, Duse had disappeared. Helen and Désirée, after searching for her in vain, did their best to soothe some badly ruffled feelings. They had no difficulty with those who loved Duse and knew her well—they were familiar with those sudden moods. But there were many who resented her behaviour as "outrageous," and no doubt contributed their little share to the stories of her "eccentricities."

Later that evening, when the guests had departed and all was quiet again, Duse crept back to the house. "Suddenly I couldn't!" she explained. "I couldn't face them! I know I'm a monster but, God forgive me, I couldn't help it. One of my black moods came over me, and I wasn't fit to face a living soul!"

These are only a few of the many glimpses of Duse I owe to Helen Lohman. I once asked her whether Duse found it difficult to live such a different kind of life—whether she ever missed the stage.

"I think she missed the *work* sometimes," she

answered; "the creative side of the theatre, which had absorbed her for so many years. She certainly never missed the externals; what people think of as the 'glamour' and 'excitement' of the stage. She was happy to escape all that. But the habit of work was strong in her; since early childhood the forces of her being had been so channeled—so focussed on a specific goal. I believe there were times when she felt a sense of loss—a kind of emptiness. Once she said to me: 'I've spent my life trying to perfect my art; now it's time I tried to perfect myself.' She was terribly aware, cruelly so, of her shortcomings as a human being, and tormented herself by dwelling on what she called the 'wicked' things in her past. She refused to listen when I reminded her of all the great and good things."

"Great and good"—these two words, Helen felt, best described Eleonora Duse. She did not overlook her faults, but regarded them as superficial flaws in an otherwise generous and noble nature. And she, too, spoke of her strength—a "healing strength, Helen called it. It was this strength in Duse—a power to inspire others with the courage to overcome—that helped Helen Lohman to start on a new career. She became a highly successful photographer; for many years her pictures were in great demand, and she was on the staff of several important American publications.

There were other times when Helen went to stay

with Duse—though only briefly. But it was this first long visit she usually dwelt on. She called it "the visit that saved my life."

Désirée was certainly right when she said to me in Asolo that I had experienced Duse's "generosity of spirit."

If anyone had told me, that afternoon in London when I left the theatre after seeing Duse play for the first time, and walked for hours in a kind of daze of exaltation, that one day she would actually send for me, encourage me, and take an interest in my work, I should never have believed it.

She never would have done this, or even been aware of my existence, had it not been for the words *"Force et Confiance."*[3] These were her own words; she had written them on a photograph of herself, many years before. I had seen a reproduction of this picture, and the inscription *"Je vous souhaite force et confiance de vivre"*[4] had made a deep impression on me. The signature—Eleonora Duse—conveyed very little; I had heard she was a great actress, but I knew nothing beyond that.

Then, suddenly, after I saw her act that afternoon, she became to me the incarnation of everything that the theatre, in its very highest form, could be. Like Lugné-Poë: "I knew then that I had been right."

[3] Strength and faith.
[4] I wish you strength and faith to live.

The dream had become reality. I felt the need to reach out to her in thanks. It would never have occurred to me to try to see her, but I sent some flowers, and on my card I wrote: *"Vous m'avez donné force et confiance de vivre."*[5]

From London I had to go to Paris. Molyneux was making my costumes for *The Swan*, and needed me for fittings. A few days after I arrived, I heard that Madame Duse was in Paris, staying at the Hôtel Regina. The following afternoon I went there to leave some pansies—flowers which, someone had told me, Duse particularly liked.

There was a lady standing by the concierge's desk, and when I gave him the flowers, he handed them to her. I turned to leave, but the lady stopped me and asked: "Did you send some pansies to Madame in London?" I nodded "Yes," and she went on: "Then your name is Le Gallienne, no? The message you sent pleased Madame enormously. I think she might like to see you. She is very tired today, but wait here a moment, I'll go and see."

A few minutes later she came back, and handed me a note. I opened it and read: *"Merci pour vos bonnes paroles; merci pour les fleurs. Regrette aujourd'hui impossible—peut-être demain. E. Duse."*[6]

[5] You have given me strength and faith to live.
[6] Thank you for your good words; thank you for the flowers. Regret today impossible—perhaps tomorrow. E. Duse.

Désirée—for, of course, it was she—told me to return the next day, but she warned me that Duse was far from well; the doctors had advised her to go to Switzerland for a complete rest before attempting to play again, and she might be leaving in the morning. In that case she would hope to see me in New York, as the American engagement was now definite.

I did return the next day, but Duse had already left.

Duse arrived in New York a few days before the opening of *The Swan*, which took place on October 24th. Knowing that she was to open at the Metropolitan Opera House on October 29th, I naturally made no attempt to see her.

I was in a frenzy of nerves the day of the 24th, and decided to try and walk myself into a calmer frame of mind. I walked all the way from Eighth Street to Central Park; then, remembering that Duse was staying at the old Majestic at Central Park West and 72nd Street, I bought some flowers and went there to leave them for her. I thought if I could be in the same building with her, even for a moment, I might feel better. "Ah, Youth! Youth!" as Tchekov says.

As I stood in the lobby, Désirée stepped out of the elevator. She recognized me and came over to me. "Madame Duse has read in the papers of your opening tonight," she said. "She has been thinking of you, and I know she wishes you success."

I went home and tried to rest. It didn't seem possible that Duse should have thought of me; but Désirée had said so. It occurred to me she might just have said it out of kindness; still, the mere idea that it *might* be true filled me with comfort.

There was a ring at the door; I went to open it and, to my surprise, Désirée was standing in the hall. She seemed quite agitated: "Madame was very cross with me for not taking you up to see her," she said. "Will you come back with me now, at once? She wants to talk to you. But in case you can't come, she sent this letter."

Duse had written: "*Chère, belle enfant, Chère Artiste qui est en peine pour son Art! Je voudrais tant vous consoler vous—dire d'être SURE de vous-même. Je me gronde de ne pas venir à votre recherche—et je n'ose pas sortir de cette chambre! Pardonnez—et soyez heureuse. 'E nella Luce.' Eleonora Duse.*"[7]

It seemed impossible. I was speechless with wonder at such kindess. Without a word I followed Désirée downstairs and into the waiting taxi.

When we entered Duse's sitting room at the Hotel Majestic, she was seated at a table by the window

[7] Dear, beautiful child, Dear Artist who is suffering for her Art! I would so like to console you—tell you to be SURE of yourself. I scold myself for not coming to find you—and I dare not leave this room! Forgive—and be happy. 'You are in the Light.' Eleonora Duse.

talking to a young man who sat opposite her. She got up when she saw me and graciously dismissed him. He kissed her hand and left.

Duse came over to me with hands outstretched; her eyes looked straight into mine, as though searching for something in me. I couldn't speak. She said nothing either, but, still holding my hands, she drew me down beside her on the sofa. We were silent for a few moments, while she continued to examine me with that kind, searching look. Then she smiled: *"Vous avez l'air d'une jeune fille de Venise,"* she said, *"avec ce châle noir. Et maintenant, dites-moi: où avez-vous trouvé ces mots Force et Confiance?"*[8]

"Mais c'est vous qui me les avez donné, Madame,"[9] I answered; and I told her of seeing them written on her picture. *"C'est étrange! Et vous me les rendez, juste au moment où j'en ai si besoin!"*[1]

She sat thinking for a moment. *"Un plein cercle,"*[2] she said. She stroked my hand for a while in silence. I thought to myself: "With her, one is not afraid of silence."

Her quietness, the touch of her hands, the grace

[8] You look like a young Venetian girl . . . with that black shawl. And now, tell me: Where did you find those words Strength and Faith?
[9] But it was you who gave them to me, madame.
[1] How strange! And you give them back to me, just at the moment when I have such need of them.
[2] A full circle.

that radiated from her put me at my ease; I felt warm and relaxed.

There was nothing about her of the actress; no trace of self-consciousness, no stress, no artificiality of any kind. She treated me as an equal; she asked me a great many things about myself, and seemed genuinely interested in the answers. She spoke of "our work," as though we were two colleagues who should understand and help each other. There was not a hint of the slightly patronizing attitude I had sensed in the other great actors I had met from time to time. She never said a word about herself; it was as though her one desire was to comfort me and give me courage. By some magic she succeeded in dispelling the fear and tenseness that had tormented me all day.

When it was time for me to leave for the theatre, she took my hand and led me down the long, old-fashioned corridor; she stood with me by the elevator and, as I stepped into it, she called out: *"Force et Confiance! Vous allez bien jouer ce soir—je le sais!"*[3]

I was able to play that night without the paralyzing fear of failure, the self-centred longing for personal success, that had so often made my opening-night performances disastrous. I was nervous, of course; but I was too grateful, too excited, too penetrated by the power of that extraordinary being, to give any thought

[3] Strength and Faith! You will play well tonight—I know it!

to self; and this gave me a freedom I had never before experienced on the stage.

The next morning, when I read the notices, I was happy because they were all splendid, but somehow they didn't seem to matter quite as much as usual. My meeting with Duse seemed like a dream. But that afternoon she called me up; it seemed incredible to be hearing her voice over the telephone! She wanted to tell me how pleased she was about the good reviews: *"Vous voyez! J'avais raison—vous avez bien joué!"*[4] But she wanted to know how I myself felt about the performance. Had I been happy? She wanted to see me and hear all about it.

During the following weeks, while Duse was playing in New York, I saw her frequently. I shall try and give a few glimpses of these visits—to describe them all in detail would be tedious.

The day before her opening I went to see her, and found her sitting in her bedroom, on a straight chair facing into a corner of the room. She got up when I came in and explained that she had been sitting like that for several hours, *"en prière,"* she said. *"Je tâche de m'oublier—de me libérer de moi-même. . . . Ainsi j'aurais peut-être moins peur."*[5]

[4] You see! I was right—you played well!
[5] In prayer. . . . I'm trying to forget myself—to free myself from self. . . . That way, perhaps I won't be so afraid.

"How could she be afraid!" I thought. But she was; and, to her, fear was a form of vanity.

Another time, the day after she had played her first matinee performance at the Century, she told me how happy it had made her to see *"ces jeunes visages"* —those young faces—lifted up toward her on her entrance in *The Lady from the Sea*. I remember the entire audience rose when she came on the stage and we, on the first row, were within a few feet of her, so she must have been able to see us clearly. *"Mais vous —les jeunes—vous devez me trouver bien vieille! Et comme artiste—bien démodée!"*[6]

Old-fashioned! She made all other actors, young or old, seem "old-fashioned" by comparison—and would today!

I had noticed that she had scarcely any personal things around her in her rooms at the hotel; they were stripped of everything extraneous; no pictures, no flowers, very few books. One day I brought her an old copy of Dante I was very fond of; it was a seventeenth-century edition in its original binding. I thought she might like to have it with her in those stark surroundings; it didn't occur to me then that the starkness might have been deliberate. She seemed pleased and caressed the book lovingly, like an old friend. "Dante! . . . Dante!" she kept repeating. She turned to the

[6] But you—the young ones—you must find me very old! And as an actress very old-fashioned!

Paradiso, serched for a passage, and said: *"Ecoutez ce qu'il dit. Il faudrait s'en souvenir!"*[7] And she read:

> *"Lume non e, se non ven dal sereno*
> *Che non si turba mai. . . ."*[8]

"Il a raison; mais . . . la sérénité! . . . Bien difficile!"[9]

Another thing I noticed was that there were no mirrors anywhere—not even in her bedroom. Most other actresses I'd known—and actors too!—would have seemed lost without a mirror. Their conversations were mostly focussed on the mirror instead of on the person they were talking to. And, while they seemed to listen, they peered at themselves in the glass, as though studying their own reactions. They "listened" with only half a mind. With Duse it was different. When she listened her eyes never left your face. It was as though she not only heard the words, but weighed the thoughts behind them. You felt it would be impossible to lie to her. The undivided attention she gave you was part of her extraordinary charm. There was something childlike about it—something almost touching; also something immensely flattering,

[7] Listen to what he says. One should remember it!
[8] There is no light unless from that
Serene which never is disturbed. . . .
[9] He is right; but . . . serenity! . . . Very difficult!

of course—dangerously so, perhaps; for it made you feel you really mattered to her.

She was appalled when she discovered I played in *The Swan* eight times a week. *"Mais c'est barbare! Vous devriez refuser,"*[1] she said. "I should like to see dear Gilbert Miller's face if I attempted such a thing," I answered. "Oh! *Ces négriers!*"[2] she cried. I explained that it was the custom in this country, that everyone played the same thing eight times a week. But this did not satisfy her. *"Non, non, non! Chère petite Le Gallienne, vous allez tuer votre âme!"*[3] Then she was silent for a moment and suddenly burst out: *"Tenez! Allez chez les Russes! C'est ça! Quittez tout et joignez-vous aux Russes. Ce sont les seuls vrais!"*[4] She was referring to the Moscow Art Theatre, whose work she greatly admired. I laughed and said I didn't think I could; my mother would certainly not approve of that!

The next day, when I arrived, she greeted me apologetically: *"Je suis folle—ne m'écoutez pas! Ah! Je suis l'ennemi des mamans!"*[5] and we both laughed.

One time she asked me what plays I would particularly like to do. I think she was pleased because I

[1] It's barbaric! You should refuse.
[2] Oh! Those slave drivers!
[3] No, no, no! Dear little Le Gallienne, you will kill your soul!
[4] Look! Go and join the Russians! That's it! Leave everything and join the Russians. They are the only true ones!
[5] I am mad—don't listen to me! Ah! I am the enemy of mamas!

answered without any hesitation: I gave her quite a list! When I mentioned *The Master Builder* her face lit up, *"Oui, cui! C'est pour vous. Jouez cela . . . il le faut. La Hilde Wangel est pour vous!"*[6]

She talked with great animation about Ibsen; of his genius; of his unique understanding of the human heart and mind; of his limitless vision. She marvelled at the complexity of the women he created. She called Rebekka West in *Rosmersholm* *"la plus difficile . . . la plus mystérieuse de toutes."*[7] Of Hedda Gabler she said: *"Qui est le démon? . . . Qui est l'ange? . . . car il y a les deux!"*[8]

One afternoon, at a Wednesday matinee performance of *The Swan*, it was rumoured that Madame Duse was out front. The excitement backstage was of course tremendous. Everyone was nervous. As for me, my legs turned to jelly, I couldn't breathe, and my voice became a feeble croak. The house manager came back after the first act to tell us that Madame Duse was not there after all; she had intended to come, but at the last minute her secretary had called up to say she was not well enough to make the effort; the performance then returned to normal—luckily for the mem-

[6] Yes, yes! That is for you. Play it. . . . You must. Hilde Wangel is for you!
[7] The most difficult . . . the most mysterious of all.
[8] Which is the demon? Which is the angel? . . . for both are there! . . .

bers of the audience, who must have been wondering why anyone had ever thought us good!

The following day—Thursday—Désirée called up to say Madame wanted to see me.

When I arrived, Duse apologized for not having come to see me play. I told her I was grateful. *"Mais, chère petite Le Gallienne, pourquoi? . . . Pourquoi dites-vous ça?"*[9] "Because if you had, I'm afraid you would never have spoken to me again," I said; and I told her just what happened. To my relief she seemed to understand; she shook her head and exclaimed *"Ah! Cette peur abominable! Il faut la dompter. Il faut s'oublier. . . . s'oublier. . . . C'est le seul moyen!"*[1]

That day she gave me the little book: *The Prayers of St. Thomas Aquinas.* I remember thinking, as I read the words: ". . . *la splendide clarté, la prompte agilité, la pénétrante subtilité, la forte impassibilité*"[2] that these were things an actor, as well as a saint, might reasonably pray for; but I couldn't see the relevance of some of the other passages Duse had marked, though I studied them carefully as soon as I reached home. It was many years before I began to realize her reasons for having marked them.

[9] But, dear little Le Gallienne, why? . . . Why do you say that?
[1] Ah! That abominable fear! One must conquer it. One must forget self. . . . Forget self. . . . It's the only way!
[2] . . . splendid clarity, prompt agility, penetrating subtlety, strong impassibility.

As always, she insisted on walking to the elevator with me. She put her arms round me and said: "*Ça ne fait rien! . . . Je n'ai pas besoin de vous voir jouer . . . Je vous connais!*"[3] I saw that she was trying to console me; she knew that in spite of my professed relief at her not coming to the play, somewhere deep down inside me I had been disappointed. This was typical of her awareness of, and her consideration for, a young actor's sensibilities! Such exquisite courtesy is found only in the very great.

The next day I attended the matinee of *La Città Morta*. It was Duse's second performance of the play, the first had been on the preceding Tuesday. This was the only time that I noticed a distinct difference in her playing. On Tuesday she had seemed tired, drained, remote. The flame was burning low, though the architecture of her performance was impeccable and harmonious as always. But on the Friday she played with such fervour, such incomparable beauty, that it was like a miracle. The externals had not changed, but they were filled with an extraordinary radiance of spirit, which had been missing on the previous performance.

As I left the theatre I decided to go and sit in the entrance lobby of her hotel. I planned to make no

[3] It doesn't matter! . . . I don't need to see you play . . . I know you!

move toward her when she came in, and if she didn't want to see me, she could just ignore me. But it seemed to me she must be feeling so free and happy at having played like that, she might want to talk a little. So I waited.

This lower lobby was like a long, wide corridor, with benches lining either side; it led to the main lounge of the hotel. As I sat there three elderly ladies came in from the street and passed me on the way to the elevators in the rear; one of them was an actress, a rather disagreeable woman, whom I knew slightly. She stopped when she saw me and said: "I hope you are not waiting to see Madame Duse. She doesn't like seeing strangers after a performance. *We* are having tea with her." I said I didn't intend to try to talk to Madame Duse, but I felt I was doing no harm in sitting there. "Well! You've been warned!" she snapped, and in a moment she and her friends disappeared into the elevator.

Twenty minutes later Duse came in through the revolving door. She was alone and had evidently walked the ten blocks from the theatre. She came in very quietly; she looked quite gay and was carrying a large bunch of red roses. I sat very still watching her. At first I thought she wasn't going to see me, but she suddenly looked in my direction and her face lit up with pleasure. She came and sat down beside me on the bench: "*Chère petite Le Gallienne! Comme je*

suis heureuse de vous voir!"[4] After we had talked for
several minutes, and I had tried to thank her for the
joy she had given me that afternoon, I reminded her
that she had a tea party. "*Oh! Elles peuvent attendre!
Ce sont trois vieilles-filles anglaises; j'ai promis. . . .
et j'irai, j'irai . . . mais d'abord causons un peu!*"[5] I
wondered what my sour friend would say to that!

A little later a group of ladies came from the main
lobby on their way to the street. They carried pro-
grammes and had evidently attended Duse's matinee.
Suddenly one of them caught sight of her and bore
down on her with shrill cries of delight. Duse immediately rose and bowed graciously. The lady clasped
her hand. "Tell her I've waited all my life to shake
her hand," she said to me. "What an honour! Tell her
I'm one of her most ardent admirers!" I translated,
and Duse smiled and bowed her thanks. The lady
turned to leave and for the first time looked at me;
she burst out: "But . . . aren't you . . . ?" Duse
saw by her expression that she had recognized me; she
put her hand on my shoulder and gently pushed me forward saying: "*Oui, oui! C'est votre Le Gallienne!*" and
the look on her face was so full of delight—almost of
pride—that tears came to my eyes.

[4] Dear little Le Gallienne! How happy I am to see you!
[5] Oh! They can wait! They are three old maids, three English
women; I promised . . . and I'll go, I'll go . . . but first
let's talk a bit!

The other ladies came up and joined in the compliments and handshakes, then, with many bows and smiles they flocked out to their waiting cars.

Duse saw that I was deeply moved and incapable of speech. She put her arm round me and for a moment held me close; then, to put me at my ease, she burst into one of her childlike peals of laughter, and cried, pointing in the direction of the disappearing ladies: *"C'est notre publique! Ce sont elles qui nous donnent notre pain—il faut bien être polies!"*[6] And we laughed like two conspirators.

Ah, her goodness, her simple kindness, her understanding, her wisdom, her grace of body and spirit, her exquisite courtesy; and then the warm humour, the sense of fun—the combination, as in Tchekov, of the comic, as well as the tragic, sense of life. How can I ever forget, how cease to be thankful for the privilege of being near her, however briefly. How can I ever forget those talks; their importance to me did not grow less with the passage of time—quite the contrary. There were so many things she said that I was not yet mature enough to understand. But they were stored up in my mind and, gradually, as I developed in my work, as life sharpened my perception, their meaning grew progressively clear to me. When Duse left New York and went on tour, she used to send me telegrams from

[6] That's our public. They give us our bread and butter—one has to be polite!

time to time—challenging messages that spurred me on and gave me courage : *"Vous trouverez une nouvelle force dans le nouvel effort."* . . . *"Très heureuse vous retrouver en pleine bataille. Tout sera bien. . . ."*[7] Precious messages that were sorely missed after her death. But, as she used to say, *"Les morts aident les vivants"*[8]—and I have sometimes felt that the memory of the things she said to me, some of them buried deep in my subconscious mind for many years, came to the surface, as I needed them, like messages from another world.

[7] You will find a new strength in the new effort. . . . Very happy to find you again in full battle. . . . All shall be well.
[8] The dead help the living.

V

AMONG THE GREAT ACTORS I HAVE SEEN PLAY, not one could, in my opinion, be compared with Eleonora Duse. She was totally different from all others.

The first play I saw her in was *Così Sia*. She was on the stage at the rise of the curtain. The moment I heard her voice and saw that frail, yet curiously strong, ageless body—imbued with such intense inner vitality that it seemed to shine with light—I knew I was in the presence of a master who had achieved absolute perfection.

The voice was not an actor's voice, though it carried, as though by magic, and without the slightest trace of "projection," to the very last rows of the vast theatre. It was the voice of a human being. Like everything else about Duse it was completely natural; not the kind of pseudo-naturalness acquired in classroom or studio, but true naturalness, which can come only from an acute awareness of nature itself.

Huneker writes of Duse's acting: "She is the exponent of an art that is baffling in its coincidence with nature. From nature what secret accents has this Italian woman not overheard?—Secrets that she embodies in her art." As she herself once said: "If the sight of the blue skies fills you with joy, if a blade of grass has power to move you, rejoice, for your soul is alive."

She was not only keenly aware of nature, but was obedient to its mysterious rhythm. There is always harmony in the movements of human beings, as long as they are unaware of being watched; it is self-consciousness that breaks it. Observe a group of children, a crowd of workmen; their bodies fall naturally into perfectly balanced and harmonious patterns—until they feel your eyes upon them: then the pattern becomes contrived, unreal. They cease to *be*, and start to *act*. Duse, on the stage, seemed oblivious of being watched; this was one of the secrets of her naturalness. As Symons says: "She let us overlook her, with an unconsciousness which study had formed into a second nature."

"Study," yes, for her naturalness was the result of highly disciplined craftsmanship.

Duse's extraordinary technique was based on the gruelling, unrelenting work of her early years. Only through acting can one learn to act; acting before audiences of every conceivable type, under every conceivable circumstance. The harder the conditions to be overcome, at least during the probationary years, the better. Duse had succeeded in making of her body an instrument capable of responding effortlessly to the slightest shade of thought and feeling. All her movements, the tones of her voice, the gestures of her hands, seemed the inevitable outcome of the moods and emotions of the character she was portraying. Once she had forged this perfect instrument on which she could rely, once she had gained complete control of all the externals of her art, she was free to forget them, and could concentrate on perfecting the hidden, more mysterious, facets of her craft: the means of bringing about, in herself, the actual thoughts and passions of the women she gave life to on the stage, secure in the knowledge that these thoughts and passions would be unerringly communicated.

An actor may be in full command of his external resources, but if he is unable to evoke within himself the various emotional states implicit in the action, the audience may admire the dexterity of his performance, but it will not be deeply stirred. On the other hand, he may be personally involved to the point of actual suffering, to the point of shedding "real tears," but if his instrument betrays him and fails to communicate his feelings, his efforts will be wasted, and the audience will remain unmoved. The art of acting is the art of communication; to deny this is to deny its reason for existing. Duse may have given the impression of being totally oblivious to the audience's presence, but she was always deeply aware that, in the final analysis, it is the business of the actor to convey the content and meaning of the play. No one could have done this more completely than she did. Yet the means by which she did it were so subtle as to escape detection. No wonder many people thought she simply "lived her roles." This, in fact, she did—but not in the way these innocents imagined. What they saw—which looked so easy! —was the result of years of study, of persistent concentration of a mind never satisfied, always searching, always reaching out, breaking through barrier after barrier to arrive at the perfection which, Duse herself felt, constantly eluded her: "I must work, I must learn!"

The first part of her task—that of gaining absolute control over the externals of her craft—she achieved comparatively early in her career, but the second part—that of learning to summon at will emotions which were not her own but those of the characters she chose to interpret—she never ceased to work on.

She worked to enrich the resources of her mind and spirit; to deepen her perception; sharpen her imagination; widen her understanding; develop a power of concentration so intense that it could translate a mental image into reality—could make it felt, and heard, and seen. These were the means by which Duse "lived her roles"; she actually became these women—she did not force them to become her. For, contrary to the opinion of some critics, Duse did not play herself. I did not see her as Marguerite, Magda, or Santuzza—or in any other roles she played before her retirement from the stage; but I know that Mrs. Alving in *Ghosts*, the Mother in *Così Sia*, Bianca in *La Porta Chiusa*, Ellida in *The Lady from the Sea*, and Anna in *La Città Morta*, were distinctly different human beings, motivated by quite different values, having totally different views on life; and if they shed tears, those tears did not spring from the same source. Duse projected the difference in these women, not by the help of wigs or make-up, but solely by the mind, by means of her creative imagination.

Hermann Bang, the Danish critic—friend of Ibsen and contemporary of Georg Brandes—in a most perceptive article on Duse's art, writes as follows: "Duse's power of mental concentration is unequalled. It is not only the very essence of her art; it is also—and this is what makes her so unique—the only means she uses; it takes the place of all the usual means, which she discards. Duse's performance is an act of sustained mental power. By her mind alone she subjects and transforms her body. Her mind is so powerful and her body, and everything related to it, is so flexible, that the tricks used by all other actresses to alter their appearance: make-up, tight-lacing, wigs, etc., would only be a hindrance to Eleonora Duse—alien things, that would hamper her and rob her of absolute mastery over herself. She wears the costume of the part, but she leaves her body free to be molded by her creative mind, which transforms her from Marguerite into Santuzza and from Santuzza into Mirandolina.

"But Madame Duse could not discard all the usual tricks which other actors find so helpful, unless she possessed quite unusual powers of concentration and a most remarkable body, capable of responding to the slightest impulse of her mind."

Two other well-known critics, one French, the other German, also write of Duse's versatility, though they fail to perceive as clearly the means by which she achieved it. Felix Duquesnel in *Le Théâtre* says: "A friend of mine, speaking of Duse and exclaiming what an admirable artist she is, went on to say: 'But the strange thing is that I never recognize her. Each time I see her in a new part, she seems to be a completely different person. And yet Duse never uses make-up or wigs—none of the external aids usual in the theatre.' 'Do you know why you do not recognize her?' I answered. Because it is never she whom you see. She is completely absorbed by her role. She is no longer herself when she plays a character; she becomes the character she plays to such an extent that she herself disappears entirely. You see Magda, Césarine, Marguerite Gautier, Hedda Gabler, Mirandolina, Santuzza, and all the rest of them, but you never see Duse. And her execution of each role is consistent from start to finish: from the moment she steps on the stage, right up to the final word and gesture, she is what the character demands. From the rise of the curtain Duse no longer exists. Yesterday she was Mirandolina, tomorrow she will be Magda, the next day Marguerite Gautier. She passes without effort from one pole to the other."

And now, Hermann Bahr: "When she comes before the footlights a volcanic battery of magnetism comes over you. She is pretty, ugly, tall and stately, small and insignificant, young and old, short, stout— according to the character she impersonates. . . . In this versatility she excels any actress who has ever lived. For each play she changes her voice, her walk, her entire personality."

But to some critics, "versatility" consists in an actress being a brunette one evening and a blonde the next; of wearing rags in one play and satin and diamonds in another. The more subtle versatility, which consists of an actual metamorphosis of the inner being, eludes them. Max Beerbohm evidently belonged to this school:

"I know Magda, Paula, and the Princesse Georges well enough to praise or disparage an actress' conception of any one of them. I know them well enough to be convinced that Duse has no conception of any one of them. She treats them as so many large vehicles for expression of absolute self. From first to last, she is the same in *Fédora* as in Magda, in Magda as in Paula, in Paula as in the Princesse Georges, and in the Princesse Georges as in *La Gioconda.* '*Io son' io*,'[1] in fact, throughout. Her unpainted face, the unhidden grey of her hair over her brows, are symbolic of her attitude. That Paula is a local English type, and the Princesse Georges a local French type, and that accordingly neither of them can be understood and impersonated by an Italian, matters nothing at all to her. She does not make it part of her business to understand and impersonate. It matters nothing to her that even an Italian equivalent for Paula or the Princesse Georges would be outside her range. '*Io son' io,*' and she cares not under what alias she comport herself. . . . For this actress never stoops to impersonation. I have seen her in many parts, but I have never detected any difference in her."

It is hard to believe he was referring to the same woman. Yet all of these men were writing at approximately the same period, so Max Beerbohm's remarks cannot be due to a change of tactics on Duse's part. The dramatic critic has a difficult assignment. The art of acting is so bound up with the personality of the actor that, unless the critic has real knowledge of the

[1] I am I.

craft—something which very few of them possess—
if that personality is unsympathetic to him, he is almost
inevitably prejudiced. Max Beerbohm admits being
"hostile" to Duse's personality, for he writes:

"My prevailing impression is of a great egoistic
force; of a woman overriding, with an air of sombre
unconcern, plays, mimes, critics and public. In a man
I should admire this tremendous egoism very much
indeed. In a woman it only makes me uncomfortable.
I dislike it. I resent it."

For a man who considered himself an enlightened
liberal, the last part of this statement seems strangely
mid-Victorian!

Before we leave Mr. Max Beerbohm to his dis-
gruntlement, let us quote him once more, on another
aspect of Duse's work. Let us ask the question: Is it
possible to enjoy an actor's performance if one cannot
understand the language he is speaking?

Mr. Beerbohm answers this question by a furious
negative:

"EECOSSTOETCHIAYOOMAHNIOEEVAHRA
CHELLOPESTIBAHNTAMAHNTAFAHNTA. . . .
Shall I go on? No? You do not catch my meaning when
I write thus? I am astonished. The chances are that you
do not speak Italian, do not understand Italian when it
is spoken. Surely, you are a trifle inconsistent? You
will not tolerate two columns or so of gibberish from
me, and yet you will profess to have passed very enjoy-

ably a whole afternoon in listening to similar gibberish from Signora Duse."

On the other hand, the critic of the New York *World* of March 1896 has this to say:

"You do not understand Italian? The language she really speaks is not Italian. It is the universal human language which was not confused in the confusion of Babel. Duse does not appeal to love of art or love of pretense or love of shallow emotions or love of dramatic effects. She appeals to human nature. She is wholly and supremely human. She touches that universal chord of emotion and impulse which runs from heart to heart through the whole human race, failing to reach none but monsters."

Perhaps Mr. Beerbohm was a monster!

St. John Ervine's answer to the same question is also in the affirmative:

"She enabled us to dispense with language. It was not necessary to understand what she was saying, because we understood what she was feeling. The greatest feat which an actor can perform is to take an audience beyond the barriers of speech."

By now it should be obvious that Duse was as controversial in her art as she was in her life. One can find affirmative and negative replies to all questions one might ask about her work.

Was she a "naturalistic" actress, or was she merely dramatically effective? Here are two answers:

New York *Sun,* February 1896: "One thing is worth noting in the art of Duse. She was not a naturalistic actress in the sense in which the term is abused by the advocates of monotony in stage performances. She is no devotee of the commonplace. She does not make her pictures with a camera in black and white, but with a brush in vivid colours. She gets the proper and admirable effect not with the uninteresting fidelity of a careful photographer, but with the bold brush of an original painter, who sets back the particulars, brings forward the principles, and so composes a masterpiece. It is true that she does not distort, and it is more importantly true that she exaggerates like a veritable genius in stagecraft. She is not theatric, but she is dramatic, and quite as far removed from what we call realism as she is from what we call rant."

Jules Lemaître, July 1897. Review of *La Dame aux Camélias:*

"The grief and despair of Madame Duse seemed to us much too reserved. Perhaps she seemed less true, because she sought to be too much so. It is certain that in real life the hardest blows are often received without either great outcries or vehement gestures, and without torrents of tears or tumultuous sobbing, but we believe, maybe from habit, maybe even for sufficiently good reasons, that the conditions of dramatic representation require, even in the performance of the sincerest situations, some heightening and some exaggeration. Madame Duse showed no other expression at this crisis than in her fevered face, and this exhibition was not considered adequate."

Did she "hog the stage" as a star performer, or did she allow her fellow-actors to share it with her?

Again, two widely divergent points of view:

New York *Spirit of the Times*, February 1896:

"Duse is not a natural actress like Mary Anderson, nor an actress of technique like Bernhardt, nor an actress of nature and technique combined like Ristori. She is simply a nervous, magnetic woman who affects other nervous women and some nervous men. She is to the stage what Madame Blavatsky was to religion. She is lauded to the skies for her realism, but she is truly the least realistic of actresses. In *Camille*, for example, she does not look like the French demi-mondaine nor does she act out the character. She is the lady of the Camellias but does not wear camellias. She is dying of consumption, but has no cough and no hectic flush. . . . Comparisons with other actresses are odious and we shall make none. But is this sort of acting natural or realistic? It is certainly not artistic. Moreover, it is most unfair; for Duse forces all her company to give her the stage and keep their backs to the audience and she interrupts all their best lines."

Hermann Bang in *Masks and People:*

"But what is most astonishing is the apt way in which she, around whom everything revolves, allows each actor his proper place in the over-all scheme—including first place to another actor, when first place properly belongs to him. No director could have stressed more clearly than Duse does in her staging, that the end of Act IV of *The Lady of the Camellias* belongs to Armand."

It is interesting that Hermann Bang should comment on Duse as a director. It is unusual for a critic of that period to mention direction at all, for in the theatre of that time there were few directors as we know them today. Irving, Tree, Bernhardt, Duse and, in this country, Booth, Mansfield, Sothern and Modjeska—in fact the majority of the great stars—all staged their own productions. The deification of the director as we know it was, with very few exceptions, non-existent.

Today, the most expert and talented actors seem content to accept meekly the instruction of "directors" whose knowledge of the theatre is frequently incomparably inferior to that of the actors themselves. Whether this state of affairs is good or bad need not be discussed here; but Hermann Bang shows acute perception in drawing attention to this aspect of Duse's genius.

In the same article quoted above, he goes on to say: "If she is great as an actress, she is scarcely less so as a director. One is amazed at the vocal harmony, the variety of tempi, the unerring rightness of stress, she achieves in her productions."

This same critic also writes—and I have seen no other specific reference to this—of the use Duse made of inanimate objects to stress a mood, or underline a situation: "She knows how to communicate, not only through her body and through her hands, but through everything she touches. No one has ever used 'properties' as she does. A rose, a handkerchief, a chain, come to life under her hands; and while she herself remains silent and almost motionless, these inanimate things act for her. As though by magic they reflect the slightest change of mood. One remembers, for instance, the flower she held in the scene with Armand's father. At first, while Marguerite's happiness seems secure, the flower stands proudly on its stalk, its petals stretched toward the light; but when doubt enters her mind, then fear, and finally, when her last hope vanishes, the flower begins to droop; as though touched by frost the petals shrivel, the stem grows limp, and the flower withers; by an imperceptible movement of her hands, Duse caused the flower to die of Marguerite's grief. It was an extraordinary effect—impossible to describe in words.

"Then there are the two roses in *La Locandiera*. Mirandolina has them with her on her entrance. Very logically, the charming hostess places them beside the plate of the guest she wishes to ensnare—the Cavalier. We notice them only as part of a delightful piece of 'business,' and then forget them. But Madame Duse does not forget them. Those two roses become her fellow-actors. They become her weapon, her snare, her shield—they fill a distinct role in the play. That is the interesting point: these inanimate things, under the touch of a Duse, actually perform. In *Magda* there is a portrait of the mother hanging on the wall: with one brief glance Duse makes it an intrinsic part of the action—it becomes a comment, an explanation.

"This remarkable use of 'properties' should be carefully observed, by those who wish to try and fathom the intricacies of Duse's craftsmanship."

Indeed a very perceptive man, this Hermann Bang, and one with a most unusual knowledge and understanding of the actor's work.

Probably the greatest fallacy about Duse's acting, one which has grown into a legend, and which I have heard some young actors use as an excuse for their own slovenliness, is the contention that Duse always played on the "inspiration of the moment"; that she always "improvised." Nothing could be further from the truth. The architecture of her performances was always carefully planned. It is true that, given her extraordinary technical resources, knowing that the superb instrument she had fashioned for herself would respond infallibly, she occasionally allowed herself to follow a sudden impulse, if she felt it would add to the truth of her impersonation. But these variations were slight; her acting was never based on constant changes of pattern, quite the contrary.

In his well-known description of her in *Magda*, Bernard Shaw wrote:

"Then a terrible thing happened to her. She began to blush; and in another moment she was conscious of it, and the blush was slowly speading and deepening until, after a few vain efforts to avert her face or to obstruct his view of it without seeming to do so, she gave up and hid the blush in her hands. After that feat of acting I did not need to be told why Duse does not paint an inch thick. I could detect no trick in it: it seemed to me a perfectly genuine effect of the dramatic imagination."

Shaw saw this performance in June 1895. We read another description of this same effect in a review of *Magda* by a New York critic in February 1896:

"In the second act, when after many years she comes face to face with her betrayer, you witness something the like of which I am positive has never been seen before. Mark it well when you go! . . . In a moment her whole past history rises up before her, the blood suffuses her neck, her face, her very eyes it seems, and she turns away bowed down with shame. How the actress accomplishes these things passes all understanding."

Helen Lohman told me that when she saw Duse play *Magda* in 1908, just before her retirement from the stage, she saw the same thing happen.

These three instances are surely proof enough that this was no "inspiration of the moment," but rather a carefully planned and brilliantly executed effect.

It has been said, and it is difficult to see how in this kind of acting it could be otherwise, that some of Duse's performances were greatly inferior to others. The famous French critic, Adolphe Brisson, explains this very well:

"I do not believe she improvises—or certainly far less than people imagine. The amazing truth of her acting is the fruit of attentive, patient effort, and it is only because her craftsmanship is so extraordinary, that she succeeds in hiding it. But to this technical science, which she has consciously acquired and which she uses with such astonishing virtuosity, this rare woman adds the faculty of really living the passions and emotions of the characters she interprets, of forgetting herself entirely as she creates them.

"It is only fair to say that this phenomenon does not take place every time she plays; it varies in intensity, it depends on the actress's mood, on the state of her nerves, on an incident—sometimes quite trivial—which has agitated and disturbed her before going on the stage. Sometimes Duse plays with her heart, occasionally on her technique alone; she 'forgets herself' entirely, or she only partly 'forgets herself.' In the latter case she is good (for she could never be bad) ; but in the former case she is incomparable, not to say sublime. She herself is well aware of this. She judges herself quite impartially. After a performance that has pleased her, she is radiant: she had succeeded in 'forgetting self'; but sometimes she is furious, and filled with disgust with her own work and the theatre generally; those are the times when 'forgetfulness of self' eluded her."

Surely this kind of variation was inevitable. I myself observed it once, in the two performances of *La Città Morta* I have referred to. Duse's acting, at its greatest, was the result of a supreme psychic effort. It is not surprising that she could not always, automatically, command this kind of spiritual concentration; this intense focussing of the mind on the elimination of self. I realize now what she meant when she said to me, *"Vous allez tuer votre âme."* If one could act as she did, this would indeed be true; and this, of course, is why she never played more than four or five performances a week, even at the height of her powers. Had she done so, she would either have destroyed herself, or she would have had to be content with playing more of her performances "on technique alone," and she refused to face the unhappiness this caused her.

It might be thought that the intense concentration required by Duse's kind of playing would cause her to stay aloof from her fellow-actors during a performance, to hide herself away in strictly guarded privacy until just before her entrance. This was not her way, however. There was no trace of "artiness" in her nature, not a vestige of the kind of pretentiousness or self-importance which often marks the behaviour of lesser actors, who make a great business of "preparing themselves" for their roles. She was too great a craftsman to indulge in ostentatious humbug. Duse's "preparation" was an intensely personal matter; it took place invisibly, within herself. Actually it was a continuous process which lasted all her life.

Désirée once told me that Duse thought of herself as part of a "working team," and this was reflected in her attitude backstage. It is typical that she seldom, if ever, referred to her "art," but always to "the work." Nothing escaped her during a performance. She might be sitting quietly in the wings—she was always very quiet, Désirée said—seemingly lost in thought; but if anything went wrong, if the smallest problem arose, she was quick to offer her assistance. On one thing she was adamant: only those directly connected with the work were allowed behind the scenes. If the presence of an "outsider" was suspected, Duse would shut herself in her dressing room until the intruder was removed. But with her fellow-workers, according to Désirée, she was simple, courteous and helpful, as befitted a member of the "team." But she hated to "talk shop," and outside the theatre, except during rehearsals, she saw very little of them.

A woman reporter for the New York *World*, wishing to write a story on "Eleonora Duse behind the scenes," managed to get herself engaged as a "super" for a performance of *Cavalleria Rusticana*. This was in 1896. No one suspected this woman was a journalist; all evening she was terrified, she says, lest somehow Duse should discover her identity. But her ruse succeeded, and the next day her article appeared. Some of her remarks are interesting and amusing, and corroborate the things Désirée told me:

"If there had been signs posted 'None but the star allowed here,' 'Keep off Duse's standing place' and similar warnings, I should not have been taken aback in the least, considering the unwillingness of La Duse to rub shoulders with any mortals, ordinary or otherwise. Instead Duse behind the scenes is the essence of democracy. . . . As I waited, the door [of her dressing room] was opened, and I had my first view of the great actress. . . . She stood there arranging part of her toilet and watching her people, who were clustered within a few feet of her door. Her eyes seemed to take in everything without looking especially at any one thing. . . . During the entire evening the dressing

[1 4 1]

room door stood open. . . . Instead of sending messengers she walked around the stage until she found one of the actresses and took her into the dressing room where there was an animated discussion over dresses, carried on in French."

Then, when the time came for the performance to begin:

"On the upper right in the wings, sitting on top of a barrel, was Duse. Apparently she was lost in thought. She rested her mouth on her half-doubled hand with the gesture she used so often during the play itself. Apparently she was getting further and further away from herself by the look in the eyes when she raised them. . . . I concluded she was assuming Santuzza and imagined she had forgotten the existence of everybody else. The curtain was ready to go up. The church bells chimed. The solemn strains of *Rusticana* wept and wailed. But no peasants were starting to church. In a second Duse had roused. With a quick gesture of her hand she motioned the group to start across the stage. . . .

"After Duse left the stage and went into her dressing room the next sight I had of her was so utterly humorous, especially by contrast [with her performance], that anyone would have laughed. Just within a door in the scene, at the left, one of the actresses had set down on the floor her property-basket of soiled linen that had appeared earlier in *Cavalleria*. During the last of the play I wandered down that side, and there, close to the door, listening to every word, was the great actress, La Duse, absolutely sitting in the clothes basket that was standing on the floor. It was just big enough to hold her. Madame's maid caught sight of her mistress . . . her eyes rolled up in horror. Then we looked at each other and laughed."

Duse's influence on other actors, wherever she played, was very great. Daniel Frohman, writing in 1898, very rightly said of her:

"Her methods, free from all that is bizarre or theatrical, the tones of her voice, the unobtrusiveness of her effects, and the towering and convincing force of her creations, offered an example in the art of acting which will long continue to exert a beneficial influence upon the work of the men and women of our stage."

It is interesting to read what some of the great actors thought about Duse's work. They were divided in their opinion; those who clung to conventional, more theatrical formats, were unable to understand her methods; but when Mrs. Fiske, also an innovator in theatre craft, saw Duse play *La Dame aux Camélias* on her first appearance in New York, she turned to her husband, Harrison Grey Fiske, and said: "I must see her in other plays, but I suspect that Eleonora Duse is the greatest actress in the world!" In subsequent years Mrs. Fiske saw Duse play many times, and I

[1 4 3]

remember that she never missed a single performance at the Century Theatre in 1923. Several years later, Mrs. Fiske told me she considered Duse by far the greatest actress she had ever seen.

Ellen Terry shared this view; on a large photograph of Duse that hung over the desk in her bedroom, she wrote in her round, childlike hand: "There is none like her, none!" And to Henry Irving, Duse was "the greatest artist in the world."

Arthur Symons, in his book on Duse, quotes what he calls "these spiteful and jealous sentences" from Sarah Bernhardt's *Memoirs:*

"Eleonora Duse is more an actress than an artist; she walks in paths that have been traced out by others; she does not imitate them, certainly not, for she plants flowers where there were trees, and trees where there were flowers; she puts on other people's gloves, but she puts them on inside out. She is a great actress, but she is not an artist."

Sarah's contemporary, and sometime colleague, Lucien Guitry, does not seem to have agreed with her:

"To say what she was like as an artist seems to me impossible. With the infinite conscientiousness of the true professional—which was her pleasure, her pride, her joy—from her first entrance to the fall of the curtain, she was in her rôle from start to finish; there was never a moment's deviation, her concentration was unbroken. If the character she was playing had been able to ask her, at any given second, 'Quick! What are you thinking of?', she would have answered 'Of you!' Such precision! Such persuasive eloquence! It was impossible to believe, and yet it was the truth, that this woman, this adorable and admirable artist, knew every artifice, every trick, of her profession—for you never saw her use them."

Mrs. Patrick Campbell, however, found Duse "too sad, and too slow," though she granted her "great dignity, sincerity, and fine introspection."

I believe it was necessary, in order to fully appreciate Duse's art, to see her, not only "in other plays"—as Mrs. Fiske rightly said—but more than once in the same play. This, I feel sure, is true of any artist—but, in the case of such an original and subtle artist as Eleonora Duse, it was mandatory.

When it comes to trying to describe my own impressions of her work, I feel like saying with Lucien Guitry, "It seems impossible," and abandoning all attempts to do so.

Many of the things I felt have been admirably stated by some of the critics quoted above, and it may be objected that I was too young at the time for my opinion to be of any value. It is true that I was only twenty-four, but I had been an actress almost ten years, and already had some knowledge of my craft. If my opinion were based on a single performance, or even a single performance of each play, it might be considered worthless; but I saw all of the five plays twice, and *Ghosts* and *Così Sia* three times; also, I was sitting only a few feet from the stage, so I was lucky enough to be able to study Duse at close range.

The things that startled and amazed me most in Duse's work were its originality, its boldness, and its truth. I had never before seen technical virtuosity so perfectly concealed. Madame Sarah was a great technician, but one was always aware of her technique. She filled the theatre with excitement, but it was theatrical excitement, not the excitement of life itself. Compared with Duse's, her art was overstressed, overdecorated, overactive. With Duse, one thought of Rimbaud's saying: "Action is a way of spoiling something." She had worked to eliminate everything that was nonessential. Everything she did seemed inevitable. Her art was simple, economical, stripped. When Bernhardt acted you knew she was doing something extremely difficult superlatively well. With Duse you were not aware that she was "doing" anything; it was so effortless; it seemed so easy; no wonder so many people failed to realize the immense discipline behind it all. Yet with this ease, this seeming indifference to effect, Duse had a power that subdued an audience in a way which even Bernhardt's fireworks failed to do. Never have I known such silence in an audience. There was literally not a sound in those vast, crowded houses.

When Duse first appeared, there was of course

applause and, very often, the entire audience rose to greet her. I frequently heard murmurs of disappointment from those behind me: "Is *that* she? Is that old woman Duse?" (Even when she was young she used to say of herself, "The first impression I create is one of ugliness!") But in a very few seconds all such murmurs ceased, and the murmurers themselves were subjugated by that extraordinary spiritual emanation that flowed from her whole being, like a visible ray of light.

I have never seen any other actress with such repose. Sometimes she would sit in a chair for a long period completely motionless, holding us all spellbound by sheer intensity of thought. She did not need physical motion, not even facial expression, to convey her thoughts; she conveyed them because she *really* thought them—she did not merely pretend to think them. She did not pretend to listen—she *really* listened. Not that her face and body were expressionless—far from it! Sometimes her thoughts and feeling swept over them with a logic and an immediacy that convinced one she had never thought or felt these things before. There was never any sense of "repetition"; everything she did, everything she said—or heard, or thought— seemed never to have happened until that instant. This was what made her seem so extraordinarily real.

One of the most amazing technical feats I have ever witnessed was her handling of the first act of

Ghosts, in the scene with Pastor Manders when Mrs. Alving finally tells him the truth about her marriage. Duse and the actor who played Manders sat facing each other across a round table in the centre of the stage. During Manders' pompous outburst, when he berates Mrs. Alving and accuses her of being a bad wife and a bad mother, Duse sat quietly watching him, and listening; one felt the irony and the contempt behind her stillness. Then, after a silence, she began to speak. At first the words came with a certain reluctance, as though she disdained to justify herself, yet was forced by the very absurdity of his attack to let him know the truth at last. Then, as she began to relive in her mind the pain and humiliation of her years with Alving, the tempo became rapid, broken, with moments of silence while thoughts took shape in words sometimes difficult to find. It was impossible to believe that these words had been printed on a page and learned by heart. Mrs. Alving was *really* talking, expressing these thoughts and feelings *for the first time*. Yet, in the three performances I saw, the rhythm and the pattern of delivery did not vary. Incredible as it seemed, I realized that the variety of tempi, the search for the right word, the phrasing, the pauses filled with thought, the changing colours of the voice, which reflected every nuance of bitterness, disgust, pity and despair, had all been carefully worked out; they had been planned with the logic and precision of a work of art. But the breathtaking part of it all was not so much the planning as the fantastic skill with which the planning was concealed.

"What was so 'bold' about this?" people might ask.

Others might object that if Duse seemed real on the stage, there was nothing so "original" in that. Surely the actors of the Moscow Art Theatre played with the same realism?

In the first place, to be as true as Duse was is in itself a kind of boldness. Truth is disturbing; some people actively resent it. They prefer the theatre to be artificial. And if one goes to the theatre merely to be entertained—as one is entertained by farce, or comedy, or by a thriller—this is understandable enough. Even the famous realism of the Moscow Art Theatre did not *disturb*; it inspired wonder and admiration but one was aware that it was a "realism" consciously and deliberately pursued. One marvelled at the naturalistic "touches," the countless little details that evoked a picture of "real" life. But it was still "a picture"; it was a splendid photograph, but still "a photograph." Where the actors of the Moscow Art Theatre were "naturalistic," Duse *was* nature. There was nothing *between* her and truth; she *was* truth. She had mastered the craft of acting so completely that she no longer needed to use it consciously. There was no hiatus between the thoughts and feelings of the characters she played, and herself as their interpreter. It was

[1 4 9]

one process. In most actors this process is divided; first there is the awareness of the thought, then the technical means used to convey it.

Once Duse had built the architectural structure of a scene—such as the one mentioned above—she could forget it, and give herself wholly to the emotions it contained.

But this unique fusion between the emotion felt and its outward manifestation could only have been achieved through years of effort. Duse herself, in a letter to Count Primoli, wrote: "I have worked for years and years, ever since my extreme youth—as was only right." And this work was not only a matter of exercising her craft by constant practice. It consisted also in keeping the mind and spirit open and acquisitive; in an awareness of all of life; of all of art. She used to say: "Everything goes into the work"—and the work was never finished.

The French writer Ferdinand Nozière tells of meeting Duse at the railway station in Ostende during one of her tours in the early 1900's. As they waited between trains she began talking of her work. Nozière writes: "She told me of her aspiration to achieve total harmony; of her never-ceasing effort to realize a perfect accord between speech, mime, and gesture; I sensed that her mind was passionately engaged in completely mastering the science of eurythmics." It is interesting that this conversation should have taken place when

Duse was at the very height of her fame. She and Bernhardt were then considered the world's two greatest
actresses.

Certainly, by the time I saw her play, this "total
harmony" had been achieved; yet one never gave a
thought to it. One accepted it as one accepts the flight
of a bird, or the unfolding of a plant. Her walk, for
instance, was beautiful—not because of any conscious
effort to walk beautifully, but simply because her mind
impelled her to move, and her body quite naturally
obeyed the impulse. I remember Isadora saying:
"Never walk with your legs—follow your mind!" and
this is what Duse did.

Her entire body, like that of an animal, was
instantly obedient to the impulse of the brain. She
had succeeded in conquering all trace of the self-consciousness which generally prevents human beings—
especially an actor, exposed as he must be to the focus
of so many eyes—from reaching this kind of freedom.

The perfect blending of all the elements composing
her performance made it almost impossible to analyze
it—to break it down into its separate parts. The impact of the whole was too overwhelming.

One of the things that particularly impressed me
was her bold use of silences—like rests in music. There
was the moment in *La Porta Chiusa*, for instance, when
Duse, as Bianca, was seated on a couch placed directly
up and down stage, so that she sat with her profile to

the audience; the couch stood just left of centre, facing a fireplace. Her son was standing talking to her, his back to the fire, and she was listening to him intently. When he finished speaking, she gazed at him for a long moment, then rose and went toward him as though to plead with him; she hesitated as she searched for words with which to express the turmoil of her feelings—but the right words refused to come. Suddenly, she gave up all attempt to find them and, turning, she moved away from him and crossed the entire stage to a window on the far side of the room, where she stood for a long time looking out. The doubt in the mother's mind, her anguish, her hesitation as to what course she should pursue, were expressed far more clearly by this silence than by any words. It was a silence made electric by unspoken thoughts. It was the kind of long, charged silence that often occurs in life—but seldom, if ever, on the stage. Most actors are afraid to take so much time between "speeches." But Duse knew how to make such an effect breathlessly exciting.

There was a moment at the end of the first act of *Ghosts;* there had been a quiet exaltation in Mrs. Alving's lines to Manders: "From tomorrow on I shall be free at last—the long hideous farce will be over; I shall forget that such a person as Alving ever lived in this house—there'll be no one here but my son and me." Then comes the crash of the chair being overturned in the dining room, and the sound of Osvald's and Regina's voices. When she heard them, Duse *did* nothing; she stood absolutely still; the blood drained from her face; her eyes grew enormous; life seemed to flow out from the tips of her fingers; she seemed cold —numb. Then, very quietly—in a whisper—she spoke: "Ghosts—those two in the conservatory— Ghosts—They've come to life again." It was a triumph of economy. Again—the boldness of truth.

The final moments of *La Città Morta* were another example of the amazing power and boldness of Duse's stillness. Helen Lohman told me of seeing Sarah Bernhardt in the part of the blind woman, Anna, in this play. Sarah—as probably most actresses would have done—closely followed d'Annunzio's very theatrical stage directions: "Anna has felt the lifeless body against her feet. She stoops over the dead girl, utterly distracted, feeling about until she reaches the face and hair, still wet with the death-giving water. She shudders from head to foot, then utters a piercing shriek in which she seems to exhale her soul, and cries: 'I see! I see!' " When Anna recovered her sight, Sarah gave the "shriek," and screamed *"Je vois! Je vois!"*[2] in a loud voice.

When Duse discovered the dead girl and, through the shock, regained her sight, her eyes, which—though

[2] I see! I see!

open throughout the play—had seemed dead, slowly became alive. One *saw* her see for the first time. For several moments she was completely still, until the realization that she was actually able to see slowly penetrated her consciousness. Then she gave a cry—not a "piercing shriek"—which truly seemed to be the exhalation of her soul, so full was it of wonder at seeing, of horror at what she saw, and mingled joy and anguish at the gift of sight coming to her at such a price. Then, in a very low voice, she said the words, as though scarcely believing what she said: *"Vedo! Vedo!"*[3]

I am sure that Madame Sarah was enormously effective—she always was. But Duse gave one the sense of having shared her shattering experience. It left one limp.

Duse's entrance as Ellida in *The Lady from the Sea* was an example of that all-powerful imagination which was capable of changing even her physical appearance. The youth, the grace, the lightness of her walk! She seemed to bring part of the sea with her; the fresh, salty tang of the spray clung to her garments; even her eyes looked different—they seemed to reflect the changing colours of the sea.

And who could ever forget the tired old woman at the end of *Così Sia*, dragging herself on her knees to

[3] I see! I see!

the foot of the altar, imploring the Virgin Mary to give her some word of comfort; and the radiance of her face—of her whole body—when she seems to hear Mary's voice? The quiet resignation of the last words "Thy will be done," and the luminous smile on her lips at the moment of death?

Unforgettable moments—great, inspiring moments. As Hermann Bang rightly said, "Impossible to describe in words."

Much has been written about Duse's hands: "Duse of the beautiful hands," as she was called. But I have observed that when people talk about an actor's hands being beautiful, what they have seen is not so much the hands themselves, but what comes through them.

Most great actor's hands seem beautiful on the stage—whether they are so in actual fact or not—because they are open channels; the life fluid pours out at the fingertips.

A great actor is not confined within the actual limits of his body. He is charged with an inner vitality that reaches out across the footlights into the farthest corners of the auditorium; it is almost tangible; it emanates from him, like an aura. When he stretches out his hand it is not the form of the hand that matters, but the vitality and rightness of the intention behind the gesture. This carries beyond the hand itself. In an inferior actor it stops at the end of the fingers, which, instead of being open channels, are dead-ends.

[1 5 5]

When I saw Duse off the stage I noticed that her hands were not, in themselves, particularly beautiful —in the classical sense, at least. They were the worker's hands of a great artist—square and strong, though fairly small. They had, of course, been modified by age; but, even in her youth, they could never have been the tapered, delicate, purely ornamental hands of the aesthete. They were enormously alive, and so sensitively aware that one felt she could determine the texture of an object without even touching it—as though her fingers had antennae extending far beyond them. She used her hands a great deal, but she did not "gesticulate" with them. They were simply an integral part of the "total harmony."

Simplicity, truth, stillness, economy, grace, strength, clarity, boldness, understanding, sensitivity, discipline; the whole controlled by the creative force of a transcendent imagination, and the power of an astute and virile mind, and served by a body which had been molded into a flawless instrument; this, to me, was Duse—the worker.

V I

I<small>T IS HIGHLY PROBABLE THAT EXPERTS ON THE</small> subject would quarrel with the idea of calling Eleonora Duse a mystic. Most of them insist that the word should only be used about those people who have directly experienced union with the Absolute—or Divine Reality, or God, or whichever one of the many terms one chooses. Dean Inge, on the other hand, defines mysticism less strictly:

"Mysticism is a spiritual philosophy which demands the concurrent activity of thought, will and feeling. It assumes from the outset that these three elements of our personality, which in real life are never sundered from each other, point towards the same goal, and if rightly used will conduct us thither. Further, it holds that only by the consecration of these three faculties in the service of the same quest can a man become effectively what he is potentially, a partaker of the Divine nature and a denizen of the spiritual world. . . . Some are better endowed with spiritual gifts than others, and are called to ascend greater heights; but the power which leads us up the pathway to reality and blessedness is, as Plotinus says, one which all possess, though few use it."[1]

If we examine the facts, to call Duse a "mystic" may not seem so farfetched as it might at first sight appear to be.

There is an interesting description of St. Catherine of Genoa in von Hügel's book *The Mystical Element of Religion:*

"All this unusually turbulent raw-material was in unusually close contiguity to powers of mind and of will of a rare breadth and strength. And this very closeness of apposition and width of contrast, and this great strength of mind and will, made all that disordered multiplicity, distraction, and dispersion of her clamorous, many-headed, many-hearted nature, a tyranny impossible and unnecessary to bear. And yet to achieve the actual escape from such a tyranny, the mastering of such a rabble, and the harmonization of such a chaos, meant a constant and immense effort, a practically unbroken grace-getting and self-giving, an ever growing heroism and indeed sanctity, and, with and through all these things, a corresponding expansion and virile joy. It can thus be said, in all simple

[1] W. R. Inge, *The Philosophy of Plotinus.*

truth, that she became a saint because she had to; that she became it, to prevent herself going to pieces: she literally had to save, and actually did save, the fruitful life of reason and of love, by ceaselessly fighting her immensely sensitive, absolute, and claimful self."

This, if we eleminate the words "sanctity" and "saint," could well be a description of Duse.

From her early youth she fought a ceaseless battle to master the "rabble" within her, and there is no doubt that she might easily have "gone to pieces" had she not, to a great extent, succeeded.

Evelyn Underhill, in her famous book *Mysticism*, writes as follows:

"Mysticism shows itself not merely as an attitude of mind and heart, but as a form of organic life. It is not only a theory of the intellect or a hunger, however passionate, of the heart. It involves the organizing of the whole self, conscious and unconscious, under the spur of such a hunger: a remaking of the whole character on high levels in the interests of the transcendental life. . . .

"Unless this impulse for moral perfection be born in him, this travail of the inner life begun, he is no mystic. . . .

"More than the apprehension of God, then, more than the passion for the Absolute, is needed to make a mystic. These must be combined with an appropriate psychological make-up, with a nature capable of extraordinary concentration, an exalted moral emotion, a nervous organization of the artistic type."

And in another passage Miss Underhill says:

"Over and over again the great mystics tell us, not how they speculated, but how they acted. To them, the transition from the life of sense to the life of the spirit is a formidable undertaking, which demands effort and constancy. The paradoxical 'quiet' of the contemplative is but the outward stillness essential to inward work. Their favourite symbols are those of action: battle, search, pilgrimage."

Ever since that evening in Verona when, as Juliet, Duse first experienced the total forgetfulness of self, she became aware that the perfecting of her work was to be a never ending "pilgrimage." She saw it as an ideal which she was compelled to "serve." The humility with which she faced her task was combined with a workman-like sense of the practical means she must follow in order to gain the discipline without which there could be no freedom.

J. J. Schurman, in his book *Derrière le Rideau*,[2] gives a very revealing account of his first meeting with Duse in 1881, when she was twenty-three years old, and was just beginning to achieve success. He had seen her play in *La Femme de Claude* and, under the spell

[2] *Behind the Curtain.*

of her performance, he proposed to her a European tour under his management. This was her answer:

"Either you are making fun of me, or you are strangely mistaken. I am nothing but a little Italian actress. No one would understand me abroad. To impose yourself on a public unable to understand the language in which you express yourself you must have genius, and all I have is a little talent. Let me perfect my art, which I love passionately, and do not try to turn me away from the path I have laid out for myself. Later, if I succeed, and have gained real confidence in myself, we will talk of it again."

There is not only humility in this answer; there is also a sense of balance; a rare realism and objectivity; and a very clear sense of a specific goal, and the time necessary to attain it. There is no trace of the grasping for personal success, the haste to acquire fame and affluence, so typical of the ordinary young actress. There is a gravity of approach, a wisdom, a consciousness of the size and difficulty of the task ahead, unique in one so young.

Duse's approach to the theatre was always untheatrical. Her love of solitude, her reserve, her sense of high responsibility, her studious efforts to widen her intellectual and spiritual horizons, her rebellion against the cheap and tawdry values which seemed to her to debase everything connected with the stage, pointed to a nature diametrically opposed to all that one usually associates with actors and acting.

"En générale elle avait la religion des oeuvres d'art"; and to Duse the theatre was an integral part of that over-all religion; she saw it as a temple which had been desecrated and which it was her mission to help rebuild. She would have agreed with Bernard Shaw that "the theatre is as important as the church was in the Middle Ages. It is a factory of thought, a prompter of conscience and elucidator of conduct, an armory against despair and dullness, and a temple of the ascent of man."

It was to this high vision that Duse dedicated herself. And if she was to serve this vision, she must follow the long and difficult path of perfection as an artist, and enlightenment as a human being—for, in her mind, the two were essentially one.

The early years, in spite of material hardships, were less formidable than those dominated by all the splendours of success. Power is the great tempter.

During the first part of her career, she was engrossed in laying the foundation for her phenomenal technique; she was too absorbed in work to think very much of self. She had an instinct for truth and for simplicity, but she had to forge the instrument which could give this instinct form.

She always studied her parts more through mental concentration—through meditation, in fact—than through any great external activity at rehearsals. She would sit alone for hours, in front of an open window, visualizing each character, listening for the sound of its voice, searching for its inner life, striving to lose herself in it through her imagination and her will.

This singleness of purpose, this power of "one-pointed" concentration—of action through inaction —was the foundation of that discipline of the spirit which enabled her, to an ever greater extent as she developed as an artist, to eliminate self, and become a clear channel for that higher force it was her aim to serve.

She might have answered the question: "What mystery is there in your art?" as Ch'ing, the Court Carpenter, answered it in Chuang Tzu's parable, quoted by Aldous Huxley in his *Perennial Philosophy:*

"No mystery . . . and yet there is something. When I am about to make such a stand, I guard against any diminution of my vital power. I first reduce my mind to absolute quiescence. Three days in this condition, and I become oblivious of any reward to be gained. Five days, and I become oblivious of any fame to be acquired. Seven days, and I become unconscious of my four limbs and my physical frame. Then, with no thought of the Court present in my mind, my skill becomes concentrated, and all disturbing elements from without are gone. . . . I see the stand in my mind's eye, and then set to work. Beyond that there is nothing. I bring my own native capacity into relation with that of the wood. What was suspected to be of supernatural execution in my work was due solely to this."

And Huxley himself goes on to say: "The artist's inspiration may be either a human or a spiritual grace, or a mixture of both. . . . Some artists have practised the kind of self-naughting which is the indispensable pre-condition of the unitive knowledge of the divine Ground. Fra Angelico, for example, prepared himself for his work by means of prayer and meditation; and from the foregoing extract from Chuang Tzu we see how essentially religious (and not merely professional) was the Taoist craftsman's approach to his art."

Duse's approach to her art was "essentially religious" in the same way.

At first the process was undoubtedly instinctive. It was not until much later that Duse became interested, and at last deeply absorbed, in the study of mystical and spiritual writings. She must then have recognized that, all unconsciously, she had herself been attempting to work along similar lines.

It was Arrigo Boito who first awakened in her a conscious awareness of transcendental values. Duse was fortunate in meeting this man, who was to be the great influence for good in her life, while still in her twenties. Arrigo Boito was not only an artist, but a scholar; and not only a scholar, but a man of high ideals and deep spiritual fervour. He was seventeen years older than Duse, and became her guide, her mentor, her "saint." She not only loved him, she revered him. In those decisive years, when she was, for the first time, exposed to the hard test of fame, the presence of this mature artist, this man of rare intellect and exquisite sensibility, must not only have inspired her, but steadied her as well. He was gentle and unselfish, modest and discreet. Unlike d'Annunzio, he loved her more for what he could give her than for what she could give him.

From him she gained her knowledge of poetry and music, of great literature and philosophy; and, most important, of those spiritual writings which, later, were to mean so much to her and to her work.

She seldom spoke of Boito—her feelings for him were too deep. But years later she confided to Helen Lohman that she had loved him more than any other human being; she felt he had preserved and developed in her that innate integrity of character and spirit which, without his sustaining goodness, she might so easily have lost.

Though life separated them—and she went on to other, lesser loves—their friendship endured until his death in 1918. For three days and nights Duse could neither eat nor sleep: "Now I am truly alone!" she said.

"Il faut s'oublier . . . s'oublier . . . c'est le seul moyen!"[3] I often heard Duse say those words. It was difficult—really impossible—for a young actress to grasp their profound meaning. And it is important to remember that this was *Duse*'s way; it must by no means be taken as a generalization. There can be no generalizations as far as the art of acting is concerned. There can be no over-all "method"—above all no short-cuts. Each actor must find his own way for himself.

Many of the world's greatest actors have functioned along precisely opposite lines to those which Duse followed. Their success has been due to a deliberate heightening of their own personality—to an ever present *awareness*, rather than an abandonment, of self. To this type of artist "self-naughting" would be synonymous with a passive relinquishment of power. But, as Miss Underhill says: "It remains a paradox of the mystics that the passivity at which they appear to aim is really a state of the most intense activity; more, that where it is wholly absent no great creative action can take place. In it, the superficial self compels itself to be still, in order that it may liberate another more deep-seated power which is, in the

[3] One must forget self . . . forget self . . . it is the only way!

ecstasy of the contemplative genius, raised to the highest pitch of efficiency."

It was Duse's realization that only through self-forgetfulness could she reach the "highest summit of her art," that drove her to perfect the discipline by which, through stillness and contemplation, she succeeded more and more in liberating that other, "more deep-seated power" which gave her work the "something else" Arthur Symons wrote of.

In his book on Eleonora Duse, Symons quotes some remarks she made to him one day when they were discussing music: "I have known Wagner in Venice," she said. "I have been in Bayreuth, and I saw in Wagner what I felt in his music, a touch of something a little conscious in his supremacy. Wagner said to himself: 'I will do what I want to do, I will force the world to accept me,' and he succeeded, but not in making us forget his intention. The music, after all, never quite abandons itself, is never quite without self-consciousness, it is a tremendous sensuality, not the unconsciousness of passion. When Beethoven writes music he forgets both himself and the world, is conscious only of joy, or sorrow, or the mood which has taken him for its voice."

She might have been speaking of herself.

The number of performances in which Duse was able to "forget self" proportionately increased as she further developed the power of stilling the "superficial self," thereby allowing "the Light of God" to shine through her.

The indefinable quality in her art, which made it so different from that of other actors, became more noticeable. Such words as "clairvoyant," "spiritual," "transcendental," appear more frequently in the reviews of her acting.

As D. H. S. Nicholson says: "It may be expected, then, that in one who has made an appreciable measure of progress on the spiritual journey there will be exhibited a power of authority in certain respects that will differentiate him from the generality of his fellows. There will be no self-assertive claim to command on his part, but rather something bound up with his very existence which is of so high a character that it will command respect, as it were, naturally. It may perhaps be regarded as a quite unconscious power of impressiveness—a something indefinable which gives the impression of a strength and a fixity of purpose beyond the normal, and so impresses itself indelibly on the mind."[4]

However, up until the time of Duse's break with d'Annunzio, her efforts to progress along the "spiritual journey" had been focussed on the perfection of her work, rather than on the perfection of herself as a

[4] *The Mysticism of St. Francis of Assisi.*

human being. These efforts to perfect her work were not, however, made with any thought of "reward to be gained" or "fame to be acquired." From the very beginning, and throughout her entire career, her desire was simply to make of herself a better instrument for the service of her art—to her, a part of that "over-all religion" to which she was devoted.

But the mystical trait in Duse's nature was so strong that what started as an effort to free her *work* from self, inevitably evolved into an effort to free *herself* from self.

As Aldous Huxley says: "Life is also an art, and the man who would become a consummate artist in living must follow, *on all the levels of his being*, the same procedure as that by which the painter or the sculptor or any other craftsman comes to his own more limited perfection."[5]

To one of Duse's fundamentally religious temperament, it would have been impossible not to be influenced "on all the levels of her being" by the writings of the saints and mystics which increasingly absorbed her.

But, "when the Heavenly Father resolves to adorn a soul with sublime gifts and to change it in special wise, it is not His custom to cleanse it gently, rather is He wont to bathe it in an ocean of bitternesses, to

[5] *Perennial Philosophy.*

plunge and sink it as He did the prophet Jonah," says the fourteenth-century mystic Johann Tauler.

Duse's love affair with d'Annunzio, in which as in all her love affairs there were strong elements of idealism and hero-worship, yet roused in her self-destructive passions of jealousy and rage, and ended in anguish; she was indeed "bathed in an ocean of bitternesses." The indignities and humiliation she suffered through his all-consuming egotism and heartlessness left her wounded and dismayed; dismayed at her own weakness; wounded by the immensity of her defeat, the outrage to her pride. During the ensuing years her fight to preserve her balance and prevent herself from "going to pieces" reached a climax.

Between 1904 and 1909 she took refuge in incessant work. Never had she played more superbly, never had she received such frenzied praise or achieved such material success. During her endless tours in the United States, throughout Europe and in South America, she amassed another fortune to replace the one she had so unselfishly lavished on her fruitless efforts to promote d'Annunzio's plays. But in her own spirit she was dissatisfied and tormented. The typical honesty, the inherent sanity of her nature, forced her to a self-examination, the result of which appalled her. She might have cried out with Teresa of Avila: "What a *proud humility* did the devil find in me!"

Just as Catherine of Genoa was "forced to become

a saint" because she had to, so Duse was forced to "re-make, transmute, her total personality, in the interest of her spiritual self."[6]

But the more Duse endeavoured to do this—and it was not an easy process—the more she found herself faced by a new obstacle: her work as an actress.

To play as Duse played meant that she had to lend not only her body, but her whole inner being, for use as an instrument by the many different women she portrayed. These women differed widely in character and temperament but, with the exception of Mirando-lina, they all had one thing in common: they were creatures of violent emotions, and sometimes actively evil emotions. The danger did not lie so much in the suffering they endured—to Marguerite Gautier, for instance, this was a cleansing, purifying, fire; but the cold, egotistical despair of a Hedda Gabler, or the malignant selfishness of a *Femme de Claude*, froze the very sources of spiritual well-being.

To one who was striving to achieve serenity in her personal life, to arrive at a wholeness of soul and spirit, to become one with the Universal Good, this constant exposure to the storms and disruptive passions of the creatures whose lives she was forced to share on the stage could only prove a serious handicap.

[6] Evelyn Underhill, *Mysticism.*

Duse more and more came to realize this, and it is more than probable that this realization was a contributive, if not a major, factor in her decision to leave the theatre.

"All entanglements must be put aside and one must be supreme and independent," says Master Lü Tzú in *The Golden Flower*, "only then can a state of quietness be attained."

How is it possible to avoid "entanglements" in the theatre? Too many personalities are involved. Stagehands, costume and scenic designers, wardrobe women, hairdressers, stage managers, playwrights, small-part actors and leading actors, house managers, company managers, publicity men, even ushers, all have their special problems; and while they all contribute to the presentation of a play, they also contribute to the restless, feverish climate of theatre life. And all these problems, all these "entanglements," are finally laid before the actor-manager—the "star" —who is expected to untangle them and solve them.

Such a climate is not conducive to the attainment of spiritual serenity.

Artists who are fortunate enough to create alone— painters, sculptors, writers, composers—are not faced with these disruptive conditions. And among such artists there have been a considerable number who have succeeded in combining artistic perfection with personal enlightenment. More than a few mystics may be counted among them. But in the theatre it is different.

A player—particularly a great player—can never be entirely "independent." He is not only the "servant of the public" (a term looked down upon by many contemporary actors, but nevertheless a true one); he is also the servant of the playwright, the servant of his colleagues and, above all, the servant of his own artistic conscience. One is never quite free when one is acting. There must always be that "guarding against any diminution of the vital power" that the Court Carpenter Ch'ing spoke of.

Duse was finally faced with the choice of continuing to serve her art or freeing herself from it in order that she might search for that *"libération totale,"*[7] as she herself expressed it, which she hoped one day to achieve.

And so, in 1909, she chose to retire into solitude and silence.

"To withdraw from the world, unseen and unirritated by being unseen, his knowledge ignored; only a saint or a sage can compass this."[8]

Duse was no "sage," and certainly no "saint," and there must have been many times, particularly during the first year or two, when she felt strangely lost— almost bewildered. As Helen Lohman pointed out,

[7] Total liberation.
[8] Chung Yung.

Duse had worked so hard all her life, since early childhood; all the energies of her mind and body had been under the strictest discipline, focussed on the specific goal she had set herself as an artist. In one way the theatre is a hard task master; but in another it is a salutary one. It imposes certain obligations which one is compelled to fulfill. The actor's work is regulated for him by the dates and hours of his announced performances. Even though a great actor may occasionally cancel a performance, or change a date, this can only be an exception to the general rule; he cannot make a custom of it. The discipline of the theatre is, of necessity, exceedingly strict.

Other artists—those who work alone—must succeed, either through an inner compulsion, or through strength of character, in creating a strict discipline for themselves; a much harder thing to do.

For Duse, these twelve years away from her work on the stage were a severe test of character and of will power. All her creative force had now to be directed into channels which, in a lesser person, might have led to confusion and even lethargy.

But fortunately for her, there was nothing amorphous, nothing vague, about this "pilgrimage" on which she had embarked. It was neither more nor less than a search for her own soul.

"She never stopped studying," Helen Lohman told me: "she was always reading." When I asked what kind of books she read, Helen was at first non-committal: "Oh, *all* kinds," she answered. But, later, when she got to know me better, she was more specific: "Many books on art, on history, and on philosophy"; then, rather tentatively, she added: "and many books on religion and mysticism, too."

I gathered Duse was very uncommunicative about her studies of such works. She never discussed them. She understood "the duty of reticence," as Dean Inge finely puts it. She felt—rightly, I think—that religion was an exceedingly private matter. But Helen noticed, during that first long visit, that Duse was especially engrossed in the writings of the saints—Augustine, Teresa of Avila, and John of the Cross, among others. She had a deep love for St. Francis of Assisi; and Edouard Schneider writes of her devotion to Catherine of Siena: "One whose faith was insepara-ble from action, or rather was action, was bound to arouse in her [Duse] a quasi-fraternal response." Schneider also mentions her love for the Gospels, "which she knew almost by heart."

In later years Duse's studies of mysticism widened in scope. Since she was never bound by any specific creed—her rebellion against any form of dogmatism has been noted—her search led her to explore the writings of the Chinese and Indian mystics. They were, after all, speaking of the same Essence—only the phraseology was different.

Duse also became interested in the fourteenth-century English mystic, the Anchoress Juliana of Norwich. Her book *Revelations of Divine Love* was published in Paris in 1910 in a French translation by Gabriel Meunier. It was from St. Juliana of Norwich that Duse learned one of her favourite phrases—which I heard her use many times, and with which she often ended a letter or a telegram: *"Tout sera bien"*—or, as Dame Juliana put it: "All shall be well, and all shall be well, and all manner of thing shall be well."

One day, when Duse was asking me about my school days in Paris, she mentioned the name of Fénelon, and wanted to know if I knew his work. She told me how much she loved his simplicity and sanity—two qualities which always appealed to her strongly. I vaguely remembered having studied excerpts from his *Oeuvres Spirituelles*, but they had made very little impression on me. "You should read him again," Duse said, "he is good and gentle." It was many years before I obeyed her. I understand now that he must have brought her much comfort. He had a profound and compassionate knowledge of the human heart. He never judged or condemned, though he was always honest. He believed that each individual has the power to rehabilitate himself through faith and right-thinking. The advice he gave to his spiritual children was challenging and bracing.

"Go forward—always forward; go forward without stopping and without glancing back."

Duse would have appreciated that.

Over and over again he warns of the danger of constant self-reproach, of overscrupulous introspection. This danger Duse understood only too well.

"You must stop being overanxious; stop continually dwelling on your past; go forward!"

And, in a famous passage, Fénelon wrote:

"All our faults have their uses. There is nothing humble in discouragement; on the contrary, it is the sign of a vexed, despairing, cowardly ego; nothing could be worse. If we stumble, even if we fall, our one thought should be to pick ourselves up again and continue on our path."

I suppose nowadays such words have an archaic ring. Self-help—except in such mundane matters as cooking, housework, redecorating a room or rebuilding an attic—is out of fashion. When we are emotionally or psychically "disturbed" we seek help outside ourselves.

But Duse believed with Fénelon that self-rehabilitation must be accomplished in private, and alone.

Five years after Duse's retirement from the stage, war broke out.

She was tormented by a desire to serve, and frustrated by the knowledge that there was so little she could do—so little she could give.

She felt compelled to abandon her solitude and join in relief work in the hospitals, with the Red Cross, and at the front. She detested ostentation and made every effort to remain anonymous; she undertook the most humble and menial of tasks.

These tasks, in themselves, may have seemed modest enough—and Duse herself would have been the first to deny them the slightest importance; but in terms of the human heart they were of incalculable value. Those lonely young soldiers no longer felt so lonely when she had been near them for a while; her compassion and understanding, the simple honesty of her approach—without a trace of the shallow sentimentality which so irritated them in many of the well-meaning women who tried to help them—managed to pierce through their armour of cynicism and doubt, and reached their hearts.

These war years, during which she shared not only the misery and anguish of the wounded and dying, but the despair of mothers who had lost their sons, and the bitter grief of young women robbed of their husbands and lovers, years during which she poured out—in utter forgetfulness of self—the riches of her heart and spirit in an attempt to comfort them and bring them a few moments' respite, a little peace of mind or body, were years which carried Duse a long step forward on her "pilgrimage." The sight of so much suffering, of so much devastation and madness, filled her with an ever greater humility, and succeeded in wiping out the last traces of her "absolute and claimful self."

After the war she was faced once again with the necessity of earning her living. She returned to acting, for, as she said herself, "it is the only thing I know how to do."

She did not complain; and she was too proud to accept assistance from the state. She wrote to a friend: "I can still work, and I must. My people were poor and died poor—still working. It is only just that I should end my life as they did."

Edouard Schneider believed—perhaps rightly—that Duse would have returned to the theatre in any case. In his book on her he writes: "People have insisted repeatedly that her return to the theatre was due solely to pecuniary necessity. This is to minimize, to misinterpret, the value of this return. There is no doubt that war deprived Duse of all financial resources. Yet I can still hear her saying to me: 'It's true; I might somehow have managed to live—very modestly—in Asolo to the end of my days. But, no! One must look higher than that!' "

Those of us who would never have seen her had it not been for this return must be eternally grateful to her for this decision.

And so Duse appeared once more upon the stage: older—so much older; frailer in body, but with no diminution of her marvellous control over her craft; and with an intensification of spiritual power so overwhelming that even those in her audience inclined to scoff at such things were left silent and somehow uplifted.

She was greeted everywhere with an almost unbelievable enthusiasm.

The critics exhausted every superlative—"incomparable," "sublime," "perfect," "radiant," "eternally young," "divine"—and nearly all of them remarked that her art had achieved a new, and mysterious, dimension.

She had succeeded fully in mastering the supreme art of "letting go"; that "holy indifference," as St. Francis de Sales called it.

Edouard Schneider wrote: "A quality that was almost saintly had grown in her and seemed to vibrate all around her. . . . Her art had become a clear channel of spiritual communion between her and the public."

And the beauty of her spirit was reflected in her face. When Arnold Genthe photographed her during her last New York engagement, he told reporters she was "the most beautiful woman who had ever sat for me. . . . The bravery and wisdom with which she had fulfilled her destiny had molded her face into an unsurpassed sculptural beauty."[9]

But most remarkable of all was Duse's extraordinary appeal to youth. "There were many young people in the audience," wrote the critic of the *Piccolo della Sera* on May 3rd, 1921, "who had heard she was the greatest actress in the world, but who had never seen her play. They left the theatre spellbound, quivering with excitement, full of adoration."

This happened everywhere she appeared during those last three years. I know that Duse herself considered this her greatest reward.

Ibsen, in a letter to Georg Brandes, wrote: "That man is right who has allied himself most closely with the future." Duse would have agreed with that, as she agreed with so many things Ibsen, her "saviour," said.

I can never forget the feeling of exaltation, of "adoration," she aroused in me; and this feeling was shared by many of my young friends, whether or not they were concerned with acting.

I think it was her simplicity and truth that moved us so profoundly. The young are often suspicious of the old; they are apt to find them false and shallow. But we never thought of Duse as "old"; somehow, she seemed one of us. We felt we had discovered her,

[9] *As I Remember.*

that we alone understood her, that she belonged to us. We knew she would never "let us down." I suppose we felt instinctively the youthfulness of her ever seeking, ever progressing spirit. Like us, she still seemed to be searching for the answers—whereas, we felt, most old people either smugly imagined they had found them, or else had long since given up the search.

I am certain that if Duse were to appear on the stage tomorrow, young people would feel as we felt about her over forty years ago. They would be captivated by her magic, amazed and refreshed by her integrity of spirit, and enthralled by her shining honesty. Youth has always loved these qualities, and always will.

And Duse loved youth, believed in youth, trusted and revered it.

After she returned to the stage and realized that she was still "wanted," that she could still "serve," she dreamed of creating a Théâtre des Jeunes[1] dedicated to the development of young playwrights and young actors. Her lifelong friend Matilde Serao wrote, after Duse's death, in an article for the *Giorno:*

"They [the Italian Government] should have given her a theatre, and the money to run it; it would have been a practical training ground for young peo-

[1] Theatre of the Young.

ple of talent; she would have directed them, she would have inspired them, she would have made real actors of them. These young people would have given a series of performances each year, and she—our divine one—would have given us the joy of appearing herself from time to time. . . . This theatre was her supreme wish, her greatest dream. No one understood—no one wanted to understand. No one wanted to do anything, and no one *did* do anything. Instead, she went to Pittsburgh and died there. Now it seems irrelevant to bury her in Santa Croce."[2]

Duse would accept nothing for herself from the Italian Government; the one thing she would have accepted was denied her.

But, in spite of this bitter disappointment, she continued to make plans; always seeking to enlarge the scope of the theatre, to bring back to it some of that grace of spirit of which she felt it had been robbed.

Just before leaving for the United States she said to Robert de Flers: "You see, before I leave this world for good, I should like to raise myself, through my work—and for my work—to the level of the really great subjects—sacred subjects—to the very heart of

[2] There was talk of burying her in Santa Croce in Florence, where so many great Italians have been laid to rest; but the plan was abandoned and she was buried in Asolo in deference to her wish.

the Mystery. The theatre sprang from religion. It is my greatest wish that, somehow, through me—in some small way—they might be reunited."

This undying aspiration to make of the theatre a greater, purer medium; the fact that to the very end she still fought for her ideals, undefeated, unafraid, filled with hope and faith, was another reason for Duse's great appeal to youth. She was still, at sixty-five, as great a rebel—a far greater rebel—than any of us.

She might have used Ibsen's words to express her feeling for the theatre:

"These people [the politicians] want only special revolutions, outward revolutions, political readjustments, etc. But all this is inconsequential. The thing that counts is the revolution of the human spirit."

Duse's whole life was a challenge to youth—and still can be. "Battle, search, pilgrimage"—those "favourite symbols" of the mystics—exemplified her whole attitude to living.

"*Très heureuse vous retrouver en pleine bataille,*" she wired me from Pittsburgh, in what Désirée told me was the last telegram she sent. She believed in the duty of the individual boldly to fulfill his destiny. Her joy in life was great. She loved the world, but she felt we were born in it not only to enjoy it but to serve it.

She "made her own soul throughout all her earthly days," to paraphrase a sentence from Chardin.[3]

She was not only a great artist but a "messenger"; a gallant, soaring, animating spirit.

When she "left this world for good," we young people who loved and revered her felt that "we were about to pass the rest of our lives as orphans."[4]

Weston, Connecticut, 1965

[3] *The Divine Milieu.*
[4] Plato's *Phaedo.*